Dealing with Anger

Dealing with Anger is a practical, user-friendly treatment of the emotion most often denied, blamed upon others, and/or feared. The clear definitions, excellent examples, and straightforward exercises Sandy Livingstone provides make this at once a stimulating read and a useful workbook for individual or group use. For the many who themselves have difficulties dealing with anger, and for the even more numerous others involved with them, this book is a must.

Dealing with Anger illustrates the necessary skills for identifying and managing anger, without requiring that the reader be psychologically minded. There is no need to wade through technical jargon or elaborate theory. People acquainted with twelve-step recovery programs will find this a useful adjunct to their personal work. Anyone who can read plain English will find *Dealing with Anger* an abundant source of information.

—*Dr. Paul S. Sussman, C. Psych (Alta.)*

Dealing with Anger is informative, educational, and practical. The exercises are useful in assessing how we deal with anger. It is a great resource.

—*Lavonne Roloff, BSc (HEc), Family Life Program Director*

Anger is often a difficult emotion for women to express, especially those who have been abused. Many women have experienced violence when another person is angry or been punished when they express anger.

Dealing with Anger lets women explore the natural feelings of anger, and learn that anger does not need to result in violent behavior.

—*Lois Thomson, Community Outreach Coordinator*
Moose Jaw Transition House, Saskatchewan

Revised Edition

DEALING WITH ANGER

Sandy Livingstone

Foreword by Dr. David N. H. Block,
BSc, MD, FRCPC, BCFE
Author of **Echoes of the Soul**

SL Discovery
Consulting
Services Inc.

Canadian Cataloguing in Publishing Data
    Livingstone, Sandy, 1956–
        Dealing with anger

        2nd Edition
        Includes bibliographical references.
        ISBN 0-9681793-1-2

    1. Anger. I SL Discovery Consulting Services Inc. I. Title
    1. Anger – dealing with. 2. Psychology – self-help, anger.
    3. Emotions – anger. 4. Violence – anger.
BF575.A5L58 1997   152.4'7   C97-900863-8

Published by:
    SL Discovery Consulting Services Inc.
    16 Marchand Place
    St. Albert, Alberta T8N 1L8
    CANADA

Cover photograph by Jesse Livingstone.
Illustrations by Nattalia Lea. All rights reserved.
Edited by Judith Johnson.
Layout and production by Heather Markham.
Printed and bound in Canada by Jasper Printing.

First publishing: January 1986

Disclaimer:
All names and scenarios are purely fictitious, and are used to illustrate a point. The author and publisher are not responsible for any likeness to real people or situations.

Dedication

To my mother Louise,
who had so much love
to adopt me at age seven,
and the courage to heal
our relationship in the
last twelve years
of her life.

Her strength and courage
in the fight against cancer
inspired me to keep writing,
so that I could give her this
book as my gift of our
eternal love.

May all the angels
be a comfort to you
in heaven, Mom.

In Loving Memory of My Son

December 18, 1979, to August 30, 1997

Your birth began as a struggle.
You fought for your life three times, and came back from the brink of death.
You were beautiful—my first born. We had an unbreakable bond.

You were a happy and carefree child until the voices took over when you were only seven. You had to fight reality. You fought to fit into a world that did not understand schizophrenia. The only thing that kept you going was the love and strength of our bond as a family. We breathed life into you every single day, so you wouldn't slip between our fingers.

You did the best you could, Devon—and then some.

This year you would have celebrated your 18th birthday—but instead of independence bringing a sense of freedom, it brought you fear. Fear of having to live life more independently. You felt you just couldn't go on, and decided to let God take your burden.

You will always be remembered for your gentleness and your unselfish love— you shared whatever you had with others.

Nothing could have saved your tortured soul except for the highest love of God. You are no longer in pain, my baby.

We will always love you, and I know you will be watching over us.

I'm glad you got your wings.

You are free now, my love.

LOSS
by Devon Livingstone

I knew my loss before I even learned to talk.

My twisted mind straddled by a higher power,
whose corrupted inner self won't let reality come
forth onto his dark world of hatred.

He sees no light in his pit of unhappiness.

The sounds of his soul's muffled screams waiting to be seen and
heard by the world of physical beings who want nothing to do
with the outer self of the person within.

WINDING ROADS
by Devon Livingstone

*(With times in our life hardened with despair, we count on the ones we love for strength
and happiness, and we hope the Lord is watching us with straining, loving eyes.
Here's a poem for the person I love with the very bottom of my heart…My Fummy)*

All the roads that lead you there are winding
And all the lights that light the way are blinding
But the love that we endure for so long
Has been tested and tried again and again.
But our love finishes first on the road of happiness and
eternal forgiveness.

We both have taken a beating, torn from our minds
And our share of tears and jeers
But we clear our heads and find the eternal truth
In our soul's minds and bodies.

We thank ourselves for staying together
And in love through the road of life that leads on forever.

Love, from your first born and your eternal son…Devon

CONTENTS

Foreword

Anger. It belongs to us all, now as forever, passed on by our parents and their parents, as we will surely pass it on to our children. Shaping our behaviors as much as it is shaped by them, a fundamental part of our being. Inherited by nature and shaped by nurture. Unfathomable power. Surrounded by insulating and isolating myth and taboo, leaving it yet unexplored, mysterious. And forbidden.

How, then, do we deal with this potent force in our life, even begin to understand it, unravel its elements, overcome its fearfulness, finally to reconnect it, return it to our consciousness and control as we ever seek to be whole, complete.

Ask Sandy Livingstone, anger expert, author, teacher, therapist, anger consultant and guide extraordinaire in this continuing exploration of our inheritance. *Dealing with Anger* reaches deep inside the heart of anger, leading us to our own next chapter, equipping us with new and improved tools to harness anger's survivor force, literally lighting the way.

Give this book to someone else if you are not ready to run the controls of your life.

Take care of your anger.

—Dr. David N. H. Block, BSc, MD, FRCPC, BCFE

A Word from the Author

Dealing with Anger was written to help people understand and "normalize" anger. It is my hope that in reading *Dealing with Anger*, you will learn not only that anger can be appreciated and expressed in healthy ways, but also that it can be understood and managed as a positive force—not feared and avoided or expressed in harmful ways.

I started researching the topic of anger in 1986 when, as a wife and mother, I saw anger in my children and spouse. My psychology classes in years gone by did not really help me to deal with anger in others or lessen my own fear about feeling angry. I felt guilty about my own anger whenever it "slipped out," and frustrated when other people could not contain their anger.

As a counselor, I met many people who desperately wanted help with their anger. Some clients would admit to being so enraged that they became physically aggressive. Others told me that their verbal attacks were ruining relationships. Then there were clients who could not feel their anger because they had suppressed it for so long, yet they sounded sad and hopeless and felt empty inside.

As a therapist and educator, I could not adequately help those people because I had not explored what anger was all about myself. More importantly, I did not know any strategies for managing anger, whether it was expressed outwardly or held in. To tell the truth, I tried not to give anger much thought. Yet there it was all around me—at home, at work, driving down the road—everywhere. All I knew was that I certainly did not want to possess any angry feelings, and that I worked hard never to show any anger. I believed that anger was "bad" and had to be avoided. And besides, I was a "nice" person! I thought nice people couldn't get angry or they would jeopardize their relationships. At times I would even become intimidated by anger and the powerful force it seemed to have, but at the same time I denied my fear of it. I discussed my observations with my husband, who admitted to being very frustrated by his own anger. In fact, it was he who first expressed an interest in reading about anger.

One day when I was at the library, I borrowed some books on anger for him. The books lay there at home for only a few days before I picked one up despite my "fear of the unknown." I rationalized that I needed to delve into this topic so I could be more effective with the people I was counseling. I wanted to explore anger from an arm's length, in other words, on just a professional level. It didn't take long before I got hooked on the topic. Upon opening this Pandora's box, I came to know that anger is just one of many emotions human beings have. Anger is a signal that lets us know when we are being physically or emotionally threatened. We are all born with anger and we can't get rid of it, or deny it away. It is nature's way of protecting us—the "fight or flight" response. Somehow, that was reassuring. I could have anger and still be a nice person!

I learned that people run into trouble with anger when they over-react to a perceived threat by becoming verbally or physically aggressive, or they under-react by not defending themselves when necessary and just stuff their anger inside. I could see myself there—stuffing anger. But how does one let it out in a healthy and controlled way? I discovered my greatest fear was of allowing myself to feel the real potency of anger.

Anger is a powerful emotion, and I learned that it will not go away just because we don't want to experience it. Anger waits for us to feel safe enough to deal with it. Often we get a little push from family, friends, or our place of employment, or even from the hand of the law, to deal with our anger. But ultimately it is our decision whether or not to transcend our fear and allow ourselves to feel the anger so that we might know what it is trying to say to us. When we can't or don't allow anger to come into our awareness, we tend to blame ourselves for our anger, or continue to allow others to victimize us. Conversely, we may try to punish and blame others for our own inappropriate expression of anger, thereby justifying it.

Anger is a "red flag" to let us know when we feel frightened or hurt. The fear is often a signal that we are threatened. The hurt is usually caused by not getting what we want emotionally. Sometimes anger is a signal that lets us know when problems need our attention. We may deny anger because, unconsciously, we recognize that it is telling us we need to make an important or difficult decision. For example, a couple needs to stay angry at one another rather than face leaving their relationship. They stay together blaming each other. Or one person may blame her- or himself for not trying hard enough. In this example, anger is a signal to the couple that certain emotional needs are not being met.

As for me, I discovered why I spent so much energy keeping anger at bay. I did not want to feel the pain of a disjointed childhood. After living in countless foster homes before being adopted at age seven and a half, I came to believe two things: first, if I was good enough someone would adopt me, and second, if I just stopped feeling anything, I would avoid disappointment and hurt. I must say that just reading about anger brought back all those memories. That was certainly not what I intended. Right then and there I made a decision to cross the fear barrier and explore my own anger on a personal level first. I knew my rationalization that "I'm just going to learn about anger in order to help my clients" would not work. I could not help someone else move further than where I was in my own journey.

Dealing with Anger explores the concept that we "choose" our anger. Anger is need-fulfilling. We are not puppets on strings being manipulated by someone else. We allow others to make us angry—or not. If we believe that other people make us angry, we will feel out of control and vulnerable, thus increasing the fear. Only when we begin to "own" our anger can we break the vicious cycle of anger and fear. This book considers all the factors that can influence our responses, including early learning in childhood.

Dealing with Anger is set up in such a way that you, the reader, will start the journey by gaining a foundation of knowledge about what anger is—what it looks like and what its origins are. It has been my experience that we fear what we don't fully understand, so it is important to explore anger thoroughly before attempting to deal with it.

You may gain maximum benefit from this book by reading it once before going back and doing the exercises, or you may prefer to take your time and go slowly from the start. There is no "right" way to complete the book, as we all have different learning styles.

I have included exercises that enable you to personalize the information so that it makes sense in your life. You may want to do the exercises with your partner, and discuss your findings with each other. This is a great way to learn more about each other while opening the lines of communication.

I have deliberately tried to make the text easy to understand and have provided concrete tools for applying your anger management skills. There's certainly no point in becoming more informed about anger if you can't use this knowledge.

One final note: what I tell you here will not instantly "fix" anybody. You will be learning many techniques for dealing with your anger, but changing behaviors is a lifelong commitment, not a three-step process. If you can begin to understand anger in a more positive way and can increase your choices for taking care of yourself emotionally, then you can begin to enjoy life more fully.

Acknowledgments

I would like to thank the following people, who have helped to transform this book from a dream into reality:

To all the clients who shared their wisdom and experiences for the past twenty years, and inspired me to explore anger in great depth.

To Gary Whyte, for seeing my vision and believing in my work.

To Judith Johnson, my editor, for taking me beyond my own standard of excellence.

To Heather Markham, whose extraordinary talent in layout and design transformed my words to a visual piece of art.

A special thanks to Nattalia Lea, whose illustrations brought this book to life with humor.

To Sylvie Gallant, who is more than a friend—she is a living angel herself, and has always been there for me when I felt like giving up. I love you.

To Lynn Heikkila, my wise mentor and confidant. Even though a country has kept us separated, we are forever sisters in spirit.

To my sister Debby Sinera. I want to thank her for being my "mother" for the six years before we were adopted, when I needed one. Miigwetch ndawemaa.

To my biological mother, Gloria. Thank you for finally trusting in yourself to know that I have always loved you. We were meant to be together once again, to bond and love each other—something that could not be possible when you were a child of sixteen.

To my sister Lorraine. Although we did not grow up together, I want to thank you for embracing me from the day we met in adulthood, and loving me unconditionally.

To my loving husband, Don, whose mere existence in my life makes everything worthwhile.

To my three children, Devon, Kendra, and Jesse, who are miracles in my life. The greatest gift they have given me is the proof that anger management can start from a very young age. My work with them over the past ten years has strengthened our bond of love and respect.

To my guardian angels, who have guided me, loved me, and made all this possible.

1

What Is
Anger, Anyway?

ONE

The Anger Cycle

A lot of people I have spoken to over the years tend to describe anger as a "bad feeling." They say that they don't know what causes it and they don't know how to get rid of it, so it's best avoided altogether. Others know that you can't get rid of anger, but they don't like feeling angry, so they stuff it inside until they "explode." Some report that they "see red" and blow up without even knowing why, often placing blame on the person who "made them angry." Both methods of anger expression can lead to guilt, blaming, hostility, and rage. Many people report feeling angry at themselves for feeling angry in the first place! They may feel out of control, or like a "bad person." Stuffing angry feelings or exploding does not relieve the feelings of anger; in fact, it creates a vicious circle.

Many people report feeling angry at themselves for feeling angry in the first place!

The anger cycle can look like this:

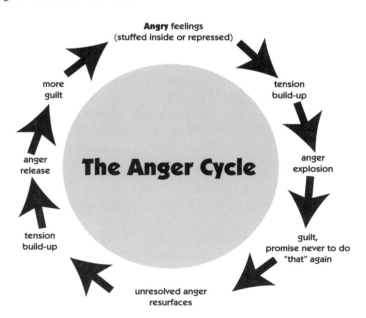

TWO

The Case of Mary and John Doe

Mary felt tired and sad a lot of the time, and often suffered from headaches.

Mary and John Doe have been married for five years and they have two children. When they first got married, they talked for hours about everything—their dreams, their likes, and their dislikes. But, as in any normal relationship, the honeymoon and intense romance are long since over.

Mary grew up in a family where everyone fought, so she made a vow to herself never to get angry like that and wreck her marriage! John grew up in a relatively normal home. He describes it as fairly peaceful, with good times. He thinks he was never really close to his dad, although they didn't fight. His father was just not the type of man to share his feelings. They talked about sports, and he helped his dad fix cars. His dad had built a shop in the garage and could often be found there with John on his time off.

Mary was unhappy in the marriage. She felt alone and not a part of John's busy life. They never talked anymore, but John seemed content. Mary found herself having angry feelings. She felt tired and sad a lot of the time, and often suffered from headaches, but didn't want to make a big "stink" about things. She knew John was a good man and a good father and she was afraid to rock the boat. She had always done her best to keep the family running smoothly and John did take notice. He often complimented her on how good the dinner was, or how clean she kept the house, but Mary did not feel intimate anymore.

One day she decided to approach John with her concerns. She found him in the shop as usual. He tinkered on a project while she described her feelings. John listened, but suddenly, to Mary's surprise, he raised his voice and told her, "You just need to get out more, that's all." He said that as far as he was concerned, their marriage was perfect. He told her she was probably just feeling overworked. He calmed down and promised to take her out for a nice dinner on Saturday night. Mary became frustrated and started to say, "But…," and was interrupted by John, who said she worried too much and she was doing fine. Mary sighed, agreed that he was probably right, and walked back into the house.

Anger arises when we perceive that something might happen to frighten us, hurt us, threaten us, or make us feel powerless. Now, the key word here is PERCEIVE. It does not matter if the event is real or not, it's our belief or assumption about the event that counts.

Mary's anger was a signal to her that her emotional needs were not being met. From what we know about Mary's family history, we can assume that she probably had been feeling intense anger at a subconscious level for some time before she allowed it to come to her conscious awareness. This is not uncommon. Remember that Mary grew up in a home where she heard a lot of fighting, probably with no resolution of any issue. So, she made a vow never to ruin her own marriage by expressing angry feelings.

Anger arises when we perceive that something might happen to frighten us, hurt us, threaten us, or make us feel powerless.

Let's talk briefly about John. His perception is that everything is perfectly fine. He is not aware that he holds his feelings back, especially negative ones. He stuffs his emotions and probably goes to the shop to focus on concrete matters rather than allowing himself to feel. He doesn't even want to acknowledge Mary's frustration, and raised his voice as an intimidation strategy when he felt threatened by her suggestion that something was wrong with their marriage. He minimized her concerns by telling her everything was fine. He did not want to feel anything negative. He has learned to numb his feelings. It may take quite a while for John to "wake up" emotionally. Both Mary and John have good intentions—to preserve their marriage—but anger that is swallowed can tear apart any relationship and leave bitter resentment in its wake.

Let's look at how anger begins in our brains, and how it affects our bodies. In order to do that, we need to step back a moment and understand anger from a medical point of view.

THREE

How Anger Begins: A Medical Viewpoint

The anger response starts as a chemical reaction in the brain.

The anger response starts as a chemical reaction in the brain (Clayman, pp. 146–147). The chemicals are triggered when something threatens us on an emotional or physical level. You don't have to think about it consciously. It's an automatic inner response that everyone is born with. You don't even need to recognize the "signal" (which is neither good nor bad), but your brain and body certainly do. This is how it works.

The brain sends messages to the nervous system by releasing chemicals called neurotransmitters. The part of the nervous system that controls the involuntary activities of glands, organs, blood vessels, and other tissues in the body is called the autonomic nervous system. This system is divided into two parts: the sympathetic nervous system and the parasympathetic nervous system. It's the sympathetic nervous system that interests us.

In general, the sympathetic nervous system heightens activity in the body. It prepares the body for action at times of stress, anger, fear, or excitement. It does this by increasing adrenaline, blood sugar levels, blood pressure, heart rate, and muscle tension; inhibiting salivation; relaxing the bladder muscles; dilating bronchi (which increases airways); dilating the pupils; dilating the blood vessels in muscles (thus increasing the blood flow); and decreasing the activity of the digestive system. In other words, the body responds internally when this chemical signal is activated and gets ready to fight or flee.

FOUR

Four Components of Anger

Anger, like any other behavior, is made up of different components. Anger is not just a feeling. We think certain thoughts when angry, our bodies react to the stress and, depending on our belief systems, we behave in different ways.

Anger is not just a feeling.

Consider the following components of anger:

- Thoughts: our perceptions, belief system, and assumptions (conscious or subconscious)

- Feelings: such as fear, powerlessness, hurt, or frustration

- Physical responses: increased heart rate, blood pressure, adrenaline, and muscle tension

- Behaviors we choose: for example, expressing anger verbally or physically, turning it inward, or being assertive

We cannot separate anger and see it as just one component, such as a feeling. As is illustrated by the chart on the next page, all components come into play when we choose anger, just as with any other emotion, such as happiness or grief.

The Four Components of Anger

Thoughts

1

Our perceptions, assumptions, and beliefs influence our feelings.

Feelings

2

We react by feeling:

threatened   powerless   fearful   frustrated   resentful   hurt

Physical Responses

3

Our bodies get ready to fight or flee by:

INCREASING:
blood sugar levels
blood pressure
muscle tension
blood flow
adrenaline
heart rate

AND BY:
dilating bronchi (air flow)
dilating pupils
relaxing bladder muscles
inhibiting salivation

Behaviors

4

We choose to express our anger "energy" by:

EXPRESSING IT OUTWARDLY
(OVER-REACTING):
verbal aggression
physical aggression

TURNING IT INWARD
(UNDER-REACTING):
denying problem
depression
guilt
passivity
general ill health
serious medical problems
obesity, eating problems
low self-esteem

BEING ASSERTIVE:
a direct statement of anger

It is important to view anger as a totality, because we can make changes in how we deal with anger by influencing any one of the four components. In other words, if I want to feel more positive, I must try to think more positively, or nothing will change. Also, if I feel enraged, I can lesson my stress reaction by slowing my breathing (my physical response). If I feel depressed, and do something, like riding a bike, there is no way I can remain as unhappy. The following chart illustrates how we can take charge of our anger (or any other emotion) by targeting a particular component and altering the outcome.

It is important to view anger as a totality.

How You Can Change Your Anger Experience by Altering One of the Four Components

Anger Component	Original Response	Typical Outcome	Changed Response	Positive Outcome
Thoughts	"I want to get even."	resentment	"I can resolve this."	self-confidence
	"I don't care." (denial)	powerlessness	"I am important."	empowerment
Feelings	rage, frustration, fear, hurt	powerless-ness, pain	less fear, positive feelings	less extreme reactions, hope
Physical Responses	increased heart rate, adrenaline, tension	stress, illness, "fight or flight"	breathe slowly, relax muscles	good health, immune system
Behaviors	expressed outwardly	over-reacting	stop, count	control
	turned inward	under-reacting	express feelings	needs defined

9

FIVE

Simulating the Anger Response

...everybody can influence the experience and intensity of anger by changing their thinking, feeling, or physical responses.

Studies have shown that we can simulate an anger response even when we don't feel angry (Hurwitz). Dr. Paul Eckman from San Francisco demonstrated and measured this physical reaction by wiring actors to a monitor and asking them to constrict particular facial muscles. Although they didn't know why they were being monitored, this action touched off a reaction in their brains that produced the physiological effects of anger. Their bodies reacted instinctively. This is important to understand, because it illustrates my point that everybody can influence the experience and intensity of anger by changing their thinking, feeling, or physical responses. Once we realize this, we have a much better chance of behaving in ways that are less destructive to ourselves and others.

The study also implies that while we react instinctively to short-term feelings, we are in control of the longer-term emotions. For example, someone calls me a vulgar name, and I instinctively feel anger. I have a choice at this point. I can go with my intense feelings and lash back, or I can choose a different way of thinking and feeling that would elicit a more positive outcome. A person can intervene at any of the four components (thoughts, feelings, physical responses, behaviors) to change the outcome and make it more positive. The preceding chart demonstrates how this can work. This is why I tell people that others cannot make us angry. They can certainly "push our buttons," but we are in control of how we respond. Later in this book, you will learn how to respond to anger with control.

Let's explore the four components of anger in greater detail, in order to discover what factors, in general, influence our feelings and actions. In this section, you will have an opportunity to answer some questions in order to gain insight into your own behavior and clarify your personal belief system and feelings of anger as they relate to your life.

SIX

Evaluating the Components of Anger

OUR PERCEPTIONS AND BELIEFS

"Perception is everything." This common phrase packs so much power. The word perceive means to "observe, realize, become aware of, or understand something" (Spooner, p. 349). How we interpret or understand the world is influenced by our past experience, as well as our needs, beliefs, values, and assumptions. When we hear a message, we often change it to fit our perception. For example, if I have been criticized all my young life and someone (let's say someone in authority, like my boss) tells me I've done a poor job, I will probably think I can't do anything right, or that my boss just doesn't like me. Conversely, if I have positive self-esteem and assertive skills, I might ask what was wrong with my work and not perceive that I'm being personally attacked.

It's not easy to change ways of thinking and behaving that have become automatic.

How we experience or interpret the environment is also influenced by our perceptions and beliefs about our world. Five people could witness the same event and each would probably perceive it slightly, or drastically, differently, depending on each person's life experiences. Many factors may influence the way we see the world: our attitudes, assumptions, strong opinions or biases, cultural upbringing, fear of authority, fear or anticipation of danger, needs, values, and, of course, past experiences.

There are circumstances that influence, or even provoke, an anger response. Some of these factors may be personal in nature, such as the values and beliefs we were taught about the world in general. The way we

11

...people tend to resist change, even if what they are doing is not working well.

relate to one another is not only taught verbally, perhaps passed on from generation to generation, but also learned through our own observations about the world. Once we are adults, these belief systems are extremely difficult to change.

It's not easy to change ways of thinking and behaving that have become automatic. In fact, our values and beliefs are probably the most difficult things to change because they have become so ingrained. One of my purposes in writing this book is to give people a chance to learn some different perceptions about anger, as well learn new skills. When we don't fully understand a feeling, we tend to make up "myths" or beliefs that explain or justify our behavior.

In my experience, people tend to resist change, even if what they are doing is not working well. We get comfortable in behavior patterns that we are familiar with, and it usually takes a crisis to make us want to change. For example, if you have been brought up with the belief that getting angry is the only way to make people pay attention to you, then you will probably continue to get angry, despite the fact that this behavior is not making you happy.

SELF-HELP QUESTIONS:
Perceptions and Beliefs

To help you come to a deeper understanding about your own anger, answer the following questions:

1. How do you perceive your anger? (Describe feelings, colors, thoughts.)

2. Where did you learn about anger? (Describe significant people and events.)

3. What are your current beliefs about anger? Are they different from your past beliefs?

4. Do you want to change any beliefs now? Why or why not?

5. If you want to change your beliefs about anger, what might prevent you from making those changes? (List personal and external barriers.)

6. List costs and benefits of making a change. (How would this affect you and others?)

    Costs of change for you

    -
    -
    -

    Effects of change on others

    -
    -
    -

    Benefits of change for you

    -
    -
    -

    Benefits of change for others

    -
    -
    -

OUR FEELINGS

Everyone has hundreds of feelings. How much we allow ourselves to feel depends primarily on our past experience and our communication skills. Even people who have been told to keep quiet all their lives can still learn effective communication skills. It does take commitment and practice, but they do not have to blame their upbringing for making them lash out or remain silent (stuff their feelings).

Many people I work with don't realize that when they continue to display hostility or numb their feelings beyond childhood, they are responsible for being perpetually angry or devoid of emotion. At some point in our lives we must start changing old, destructive feelings by beginning to trust ourselves—what we see, feel, hear, and think. If we continue to blame our past or other people, nothing will change. We will be emotionally enslaved to others.

When we feel threatened, frustrated, powerless, fearful, resentful, or hurt, we must try to work through these feelings so that we can free ourselves. For example, for years I was afraid of the dark. Every time the lights went out suddenly, I would go into my fear and panic mode. I felt like a baby. I was a slave to darkness, and kept saying to myself and others, "Oh, I've always been that way." I made no attempts to change. Finally I grew very tired of being afraid. I began the process of thinking different thoughts, slowing my breathing (which decreases the flight response), and just persevering. Only then did I finally conquer the dark. Metaphorically speaking, I erased an old tape and put in a new one! How many old tapes are you holding on to?

> *When we feel threatened, frustrated, powerless, fearful, resentful, or hurt, we must try to work through these feelings so that we can free ourselves.*

SELF-HELP QUESTIONS: Feelings

1. What feelings do you have about anger? Make a list of all the other feelings that seem to go with your anger (for example, fear, defensiveness, anxiety).

2. What feeling in particular affects you the most? Why?

3. What is that feeling telling you?

4. What can you do to change the message if it is a negative one (an "old tape")?

OUR PHYSICAL RESPONSES

Sometimes, it's our bodies that give us the first clue that we have angry feelings.

Earlier we learned how the sympathetic nervous system heightens activity in the body. When our brain gets the signal to release certain chemicals responsible for fight or flight, our bodies "rev up." But what if there is no real threat, yet because of our perception, or just habit, we continue to stay in that revved-up state? Our bodies become worn down. Our immune system eventually weakens and that's why we have so many physical stress symptoms. We all know that ulcers are a result of chronic stress. Other ailments can also be attributed to prolonged anger or anxiety states, such as headaches, chronic back pain, and heart disease. These illnesses are very real and not just "in the mind."

Sometimes, it's our bodies that give us the first clue that we have angry feelings. For example, your body probably holds tension in one particular place, such as your stomach, bowels, chest, head, or back. Listen to your body. It is telling you that something is out of balance.

SELF-HELP QUESTIONS: Physical Responses

1. Where do you hold anger in your body?

2. Do you suffer from chronic physical problems? Do you know what triggers these problems?

3. Do you easily get stressed out, or lack energy?

4. Do you keep your lifestyle in balance (exercise, rest, fun, work)? If not, why?

5. How can you change the ways your body responds to anger and stress? (Consider breathing, exercise, meditation, diet, relaxation.)

OUR BEHAVIORS

Expressing anger outwardly or turning it inward is not necessarily bad. Anger is a defense that is very healthy when it is used appropriately. For example, if you were being attacked, it would make a lot of sense to yell, scream, and punch in order to survive. If a doctor said you had a potentially fatal disease, it would make sense to feel angry or numb about the prospect of being deprived of a long and healthy life. Anger and denial distance you from the situation, and give you time to accept it gradually. Problems with anger occur when we don't return to a "normal" state. In other words, we are constantly ready to fight or flee; we are always very aggressive or very passive. Even passive people eventually "explode," because hiding anger does not make it disappear. And "letting it all hang out" doesn't mean that you purge yourself of anger, either. In both cases, if you don't resolve the cause, the feelings will always resurface.

Anger is a defense that is very healthy when it is used appropriately.

17

SELF-HELP QUESTIONS: Behaviors

1. What behaviors do you currently choose when you feel angry? Describe them in detail.

2. How do you currently respond when faced with anger from others? Describe what pushes your buttons.

3. Do you get hooked into other people's anger energy? How?

4. Do you often feel like a victim, or blame yourself for other people's behavior?

5. Do you ever hit others in an attempt to gain control? If so, think of a recent situation and describe the feelings you had just before you struck.

6. Do you save your anger and express it at people who did not cause it? If so, describe what happens.

2

What Does Anger Look Like?

SEVEN

The Visibility of Anger

Anger may be camouflaged or hidden so that others are unaware of our anger, or it may be denied by us, so that we are totally unaware of our own feelings. Denying or repressing anger can have positive results if this gives us time to deal with an emotionally overwhelming situation or prevents us from reacting abusively. Anger can take a number of forms, depending on how visible it is to the person him- or herself and others. This is shown in the following diagram.

The Visibility of Anger

Person and others see anger. Person may feel misunderstood. Person may feel like a victim. Person may feel tired, unhappy.	***Others do not see any anger.*** Person camouflages it by smiling. Person hides anger, but feels angry.
Person is unaware of anger. Others may see person as angry. Person is difficult to get along with, or abused.	***Person and others do not see anger.*** Anger is unknown at a conscious level. There may be some physical symptoms. Anger is repressed to the point that the origin or nature of the problem is lost.

Since other people may be aware of your anger, it is critical that you remain open to others in order to understand yourself better. They may offer valuable feedback that can help you begin to piece together your feelings and your behavior. Think about where you fit into this diagram and seriously consider whether you are hiding anything from those around you, or even from yourself.

21

SELF-HELP WORKSHEET: Do You Have Hidden Anger?

Check all the phrases that describe you.

_____ 1. Procrastination when asked to do something you don't want to do

_____ 2. Thoughts of revenge

_____ 3. Using sarcasm to be "humorous"

_____ 4. Frequently sounding and acting negative

_____ 5. Being over-polite, or making an effort to be constantly cheerful

_____ 6. Frequent sighing

_____ 7. Smiling while feeling sad inside

_____ 8. Frequent disturbing or frightening dreams

_____ 9. Over-controlled monotone speaking voice

_____ 10. Difficulty in getting to sleep or sleeping through the night

_____ 11. Boredom, apathy, loss of interest in things you usually enjoy

_____ 12. Chronic physical ailments or stress

_____ 13. Getting tired more easily than usual, or at inappropriate times

_____ 14. Over-reacting about small issues

_____ 15. Pacing

_____ 16. Waking up tired rather than rested or refreshed

_____ 17. Clenched jaws, and/or grinding of teeth—especially while sleeping

_____ 18. Facial tics, spasmodic foot movements, habitual fist clenching and similar repeated acts done unintentionally or unconsciously

_____ 19. Chronically stiff or sore neck or shoulder muscles

_____ 20. Chronic depression—extended periods of feeling "down" for no reason

_____ 21. Stomach ulcers

EIGHT

Forms of Anger Expression

There are five basic ways that anger can be recognized in behavior. Two forms are very visible, as they are expressed outwardly, and three forms are more hidden. Often we are not aware of our feelings of anger. Only the symptoms of anger are identifiable, such as chronic fatigue, illness, and low self-esteem.

Often we are not aware of our feelings of anger.

As you read the following, start to identify the form of expression you most often use. The purpose of identifying anger forms is not to pathologize or "label" you. It is to let you know if you are stuck in one particular form of anger expression that is not working for you. Most of us have used all these forms at one time or another. There's nothing wrong with that—there is a problem only if a particular form of expression is dysfunctional and causes pain in your life.

ANGER EXPRESSED OUTWARDLY
(over-reacting)

Anger is expressed outwardly in an effort to keep unpleasant feelings away. Let's take the case of Joe. He has always felt extremely vulnerable if he expresses his feelings to anyone, even himself. Sometime in his life, probably starting in his childhood, he learned to safeguard his emotions by ventilating anger verbally and physically and directing it at others. He does not have to "own" his feelings or recognize that he is out of control. All he knows is that to get others to respond, or to get what he needs (and to regain a sense of control), he must use anger as a weapon. But, like most people in his situation, Joe over-reacts. This is the result of fear—fear of losing, fear of being "found out" if anyone knows his true feelings. His greatest fear is that his already fragile self-esteem will be lowered if he fails to win the "battle."

Expressing anger outwardly does not work well, however. Such outbursts usually cause guilt and shame, which lead to further blame or repression of anger. This starts the anger cycle that a lot of people describe as a horrible merry-go-round that they can't get off of.

Physical Aggression

Emotional triggers:	Joe already feels unhappy, discouraged, powerless, out of control.
Environmental triggers:	He experiences tension with his spouse, children, or boss, or was caught in a traffic jam.
Anger release:	Joe takes out his anger energy by being physically abusive, slamming doors, and breaking things.
Emotional trigger:	Joe now feels guilty, makes apologies, and promises he will never do that again. But he doesn't know how to stop reacting on impulse, so he is even more susceptible to emotional triggers, waiting for any event to help him release the anger energy he has stored.

If you want to change this pattern, you will have to begin by looking at your emotional trigger(s), instead of blaming others. Usually, people who physically "explode" see only the other person's behavior and not their own. I hear comments such as "They deserved it," or "I couldn't hold it in any longer." These statements are signs that the person believes he or she "had no choice." We all have choices, but it takes a willingness to allow ourselves to be vulnerable long enough to figure out what is going on. Another person never "deserves" to be violated. Men, in particular, have told me that they use anger to get power over others. They do not see that they feel powerless inside. Powerless people try to overpower others through this type of anger expression.

The negative consequences of physical aggression include embarrassment and guilt. It can result in the termination of a friendship, which can be a gradual process or very abrupt. People who "let fly" at work can lose their jobs, or quit due to intense shame, especially if they have injured others or damaged property.

Many men have told me they "work off" their anger by going to the gym. That is a good intervention instead of hitting someone, but if they do not address the issue that led to such intense feelings, nothing gets resolved, except that they develop muscles! Other people have said that striking out verbally or physically gives them a temporary "release." That's why it's hard to stop these anger cycles. Physical aggression leads to more aggression, because after the first time, each subsequent outburst becomes more and more an automatic response.

The long and short of it is this: nothing good comes from physical aggression, unless you're defending your life. It causes broken hearts, shattered relationships, and guilt.

Verbal Aggression

Let's look at Sue. Her environmental triggers are looking after three children, working full time, and not getting out to have fun and meet her own personal needs. Her emotional triggers are loneliness and lack of support from her spouse. She feels hopeless and powerless because the kids don't seem to listen to her, and she's depressed because she "doesn't have a life." She can't yell and release her frustration at work, so she comes home and lets it all out there. She now feels more out of control, angry at herself and the world. More importantly, she also feels tremendous guilt and shame for hurting the people she loves. But the cycle doesn't seem to stop, and Sue can't get off the merry-go-round.

When we explode verbally, it is usually to keep anger away from ourselves by directing it at others.

When we explode verbally, it is usually to keep anger away from ourselves by directing it at others. We punish or blame someone else, instead of acknowledging pain, or taking responsibility for our own ineffective behavior. Sue probably doesn't have the skills to express her feelings assertively. She probably never learned parenting skills to change her children's misbehavior. All she wants to do is to keep peace and order in her house, to feel internal control—as so many women have been socialized to do. The "social representations we hold actually shape our behavior" (Campbell, p. 16).

We usually direct our anger at those people who we feel are responsible for meeting our needs. For example, if you yell at your spouse or children, you probably expect something (help, love, attention, cooperation) and are not getting what you need. Many women have told me that they feel powerless and use anger to regain control.

Verbal aggression is an ineffective way to let others know what we need. Like physical aggressors, verbal aggressors do not realize that they are blaming the environmental triggers, instead of looking at the emotional triggers. They feel powerless and try to get internal control through verbal intimidation. Verbal aggression also can destroy relationships and cause tremendous guilt. If we don't stop pointing the finger at someone or something else, nothing will ever change.

ANGER TURNED INWARD (under-reacting)

All forms of anger turned inward are unconscious strategies to deny angry feelings. Many people turn anger inward to protect a relationship or their own emotional security. That's what Jane did. She learned from an early age to minimize, repress, or completely deny her anger. It wasn't "ladylike." She learned that if people expressed anger toward her, they did not love her. Conversely, if she got angry, she would be rejecting another person. Jane had to find some other way to release the anger energy that was built up during many years of denial.

Jane turned her anger inward to get the love and approval that we all need so much. But stuffing anger offers only false security. A person who numbs anger probably numbs a lot of other emotions as well. We can't be that selective in choosing what not to feel! We may also lose the ability to love deeply and be intimate.

If you believe that expressing angry feelings will destroy a relationship, then of course you will deny your feelings altogether, or blame yourself (letting the other person off the hook), or become physically ill as a way to release the anger energy that you have stored. Stuffing anger often results in guilt, depression, and feelings of incompetence and helplessness, and ultimately can lead to physical and emotional exhaustion, suicide attempts, chronic physical problems, serious illness, and an ever-shrinking self-esteem.

Let's explore the three types of anger that is turned inward. Maybe you know someone who uses one of these methods.

Using Your Body for Anger Expression

Let's return briefly to a former discussion about how anger starts in our bodies. Remember that the sympathetic nervous system is the "emergency system" that prepares us to deal with many kinds of immediate concerns. When it is activated, the heart beats faster, blood pressure rises, adrenaline increases, more sugar is released into the bloodstream, and muscles tense. We are angry.

When we don't resolve the anger, the sympathetic system thinks there is still an emergency and continues to be in a state of alert. Memories alone can trigger this alert state.

Now let's suppose, as in Jane's case, that we are not even aware of our anger, or we are aware, but have a strong unspoken rule that says, "Don't be angry." What we have here is a lot of stored anger, but no way (or desire) to release it—until it can be contained no longer. When this stuffing is repeated often enough, it causes physical deterioration such as headaches, stomach problems, colds, colitis, hypertension, backache, skin conditions, sexual problems, and fatigue. The failure to express anger leads to increased stress, weakening the immune system in both men and women (Clayman, p. 147).

People with these kinds of symptoms are too uncomfortable or too threatened to deal with their underlying feelings, so their unconscious mind tries to do them a favor by channeling the bottled-up feelings into the more acceptable form of physical symptoms. However, anger remains as the unrecognized source of the problem.

Self-Punishing

Again, to punish oneself is an unconscious strategy used to protect relationships by not expressing anger—thus "saving" the relationship, be it personal or with a co-worker or boss. People tell themselves that they are wrong, even if they're not.

We give silent messages to ourselves every day…it seems more acceptable in our society to get mad at yourself than at someone else, even when the other person is clearly in the wrong.

Amanda is a self-punisher. She learned not to make waves. She believes that only bad things will come from being honest about her true feelings. She seems to be caring, friendly, and smart. She has a gentle manner and soft voice, but sometimes she appears to have a phony sweetness about her that sounds just a little bitter and artificial. After all, Amanda has to work hard at stuffing her feelings. She handles anger by smiling, looking and sounding happy on the outside.

But Amanda is not happy on the inside. She constantly runs herself down, feeling powerless and insignificant. She doesn't know that these inner attacks can cause depression or suicidal thoughts.

We give silent messages to ourselves every day. They are often angry messages, such as, "How could I be so stupid?" or "Why did I do that? What an idiot I am!" It seems more acceptable in our society to get mad at yourself than at someone else, even when the other person is clearly in the wrong. Too many people say "sorry" for everything, even when they are not at fault.

I'll never forget a client from Germany who, in the middle of my lecture on assertion, burst out in reaction when someone said, "I'm sorry." "Why is everyone in Canada sorry for everything they do?" she asked. "I came to this country not long ago, and I am shocked at the number of times I hear people saying 'I'm sorry!' What are you all sorry about? In Germany, we don't apologize for every little thing!" Everyone nodded and broke out laughing, but she was dead on. Apologizing without separating yourself (as a person) from a mistake you made (your behavior) only diminishes your self-esteem to dangerously low levels. This form of anger expression may be so subtle that it takes an emotional crisis to realize how shriveled our self-image has become.

Passive-Aggressiveness

The passive-aggressive form of anger expression occurs when a person feels one way inside, but acts very differently on the outside. Bill has this problem. He works very hard to con us (and himself) into believing he is happy. Bill suffers from feelings that he "should not" feel. When his anger arises, it is often "softened" by remarks that deny his true emotions. For example, you may notice that Bill is angry because he is giving visible cues such as breathing heavily, looking frustrated, or acting impatient. When you ask him what's wrong, however, he will answer, "Nothing." Bill may truly be unaware that his internal feelings are so visible. He may laugh inappropriately or, if you question the anger, may try to make you think you are imagining things and quickly turn the discussion to your feelings, rather than his own.

But the true anger comes out in an odd, aggressive way, and we feel uneasy. When you feel deflated or put-down, trust your feelings. Some people are driven to be in control of their feelings at all times and will deny any emotion that makes them feel vulnerable and powerless, even if it means insulting you, or questioning your reality.

ANGER EXPRESSION QUESTIONNAIRE:
Where do you stand?

The following questionnaire may help you determine your communication style as it relates to anger.

INSTRUCTIONS: Each of the following numbered items consists of three statements. Answer each question by checking the one response which best applies to your own feelings or opinions.

Choose one frame of reference (circumstance) for answering all questions (for example, work-related conflicts, family conflicts, or social conflicts). The reason for this is that we tend to respond differently depending on the environment we're in. Keep that single frame of reference in mind when answering all the questions.

WHAT IS YOUR FRAME OF REFERENCE? _____

Example

    a.   When I become involved in a conflict, I usually ignore the problem. _____

    b.   I respond in a hostile manner. _____

    c.   I try to persuade the person to give up his or her hostile behavior. ✔

Remember to give only one answer for each question.

1. a.   When I feel angry inside, I do not want to upset anyone by expressing my feelings. _____

    b.   When I feel angry inside, I tell the person I'm with what I'm feeling in an unharmful way. _____

    c.   When I feel angry inside, I don't hesitate to "blow off steam," sometimes yelling or getting physical. _____

2. a.   When someone I care about is hostile toward me, I let her or him know that I'm offended without feeling guilty. _____

    b.   I stay and listen as long as possible. _____

    c.   I fire back a response so the person will not try that again! _____

3. a.   When I am in a dispute, I usually to try to get the other person to see things my way. _____

    b.   I think you should keep your anger and opinions to yourself, otherwise you will only make things worse. _____

    c.   It's important to examine the issues as logically as possible. _____

4. a. I appreciate it when someone I know checks on how I feel. It doesn't threaten me. ____

   b. If someone asks me if I am upset, I usually say no or minimize my feelings; otherwise they might leave me or get angry. ____

   c. Nobody should probe into another person's feelings. If you answer honestly, the person can use it as a weapon later. ____

5. a. I often get a nervous stomach or a headache if I'm upset. ____

   b. Others have told me I can handle any pressure with ease. ____

   c. I don't let things upset me physically. I'll have a little drink to calm my nerves. ____

6. a. If I ever feel rage, I try not to let it upset me. ____

   b. I never let things build up until I'm enraged. I deal with the situation long before that stage. ____

   c. I've been assaultive, reckless in my driving, or abusive because of my rage. ____

7. a. I find it difficult to say no to requests for favors. People need me and I don't want them to get upset. ____

   b. I do favors only if I get something in return. ____

   c. I feel perfectly comfortable refusing a request without giving a reason. ____

8. a. When someone who is relatively unimportant to me hurts my feelings, I just give him or her "the silent treatment." ____

   b. When someone hurts my feelings, I feel low. I think it's my fault, or I just walk away. ____

   c. When someone hurts my feelings, I consider discussing it. ____

9. a. My feelings and moods affect my eating habits. ____

   b. I figure out what's behind my anger and choose how to deal with it. ____

   c. I go to bars or get high to let out my feelings. ____

10. a. In a group situation, I usually agree with the majority. ____

    b. I express my opinions, even if they differ from those of others. ____

    c. I usually get people to see things my way. ____

11.a.   I'm usually the person who makes the decisions and
        that frustrates me.   _____

   b.   I usually agree with others, or if someone asks where
        I want to go, I'll say, "It doesn't really matter."   _____

   c.   I state my preference, but am willing to negotiate.   _____

12.a.   I never criticize others.   _____

   b.   I make fun of people, but it's all meant as a joke.   _____

   c.   Criticism is only valuable if the person wants feedback or
        if our relationship will be strengthened by it.   _____

13.a.   I often feel powerless.   _____

   b.   I usually recognize my "body cues" for anger and deal with
        issues before I suffer physically.   _____

   c.   I never get sick—I just get even! I never feel powerless—
        that's for sissies. I take control.   _____

14.a.   I always try to avoid conflict.   _____

   b.   I express my anger assertively, with control and resolution. _____

   c.   I often try hard to overpower someone with my speech.   _____

15.a.   I think it's important to express your opinion, as long as
        it doesn't infringe on the rights of others.   _____

   b.   I think it's important to keep the peace and not argue my point. _____

   c.   I usually argue my point until the other person finally sees
        things my way.   _____

16.a.   I feel guilty when someone indicates that I've done something
        wrong.   _____

   b.   I find it's usually the other person who is in the wrong, and
        I'll point it out.   _____

   c.   I find out if I really have made a mistake, and if so, I don't
        think badly of myself.   _____

17.a.   I don't care if someone is mad—it's not my problem.   _____

   b.   I ask directly if the person is upset with me and ask for clarification. _____

   c.   If I'm not sure if someone is angry with me, I leave well enough
        alone.   _____

18.a.   I get so frustrated when others won't listen to me. I feel helpless.   ____

b.   I know how to be consistent and ask for what I need.   ____

c.   I get others to listen by yelling, or I get physical.   ____

19.a.   I often feel tired for no apparent reason.   ____

b.   I only feel tired if I didn't get enough sleep. I try to balance my lifestyle.   ____

c.   Others often think I'm in a bad mood, but I don't see it.   ____

20.a.   When someone does something that irritates me, I feel comfortable about expressing my feelings.   ____

b.   I insist that people change what they are doing when I am talking.   ____

c.   I try to overlook or avoid conflict altogether.   ____

21.a.   When I have personal needs, I use manipulation to get them met.   ____

b.   I put other people's needs ahead of my own.   ____

c.   I can meet my own needs without "using" other people.   ____

22.a.   I usually cry when I'm angry.   ____

b.   I usually talk directly to the person with whom I'm angry, or discuss the situation with someone else.   ____

c.   I usually show my anger in verbal or physical ways. Letting it out helps.   ____

23. a.   I try hard to get my way in conflict situations.   ____

b.   I usually work out differences cooperatively.   ____

c.   I am easygoing and take a "soft" position to ease the stress.   ____

24.(Answer this question only if your frame of reference is with your partner.

a.   I need sex a lot more than my partner, and I sometimes have to be pretty aggressive to get it.   ____

b.   I often feel unattractive and use sex as a way to feel better about myself, or I often feel pressured into having sex.   ____

c.   I have a healthy sex life and can refuse sex if I don't feel like it.   ____

ANGER EXPRESSION QUESTIONNAIRE:
Scoring

Instructions: When you have answered all the questions, check your answers against the score sheet below. Each possible answer (a, b, or c) has been given a score. Write the score for each of your answers in the last column (an example has been done for you). Then add your scores to arrive at a total. Compare your total with the interpretation on the following page.

Example	1	3	2	2
QUESTION	a	b	c	SCORE
1	1	2	3	
2	2	1	3	
3	3	1	2	
4	2	1	3	
5	1	2	3	
6	1	2	3	
7	1	3	2	
8	3	1	2	
9	1	2	3	
10	1	2	3	
11	3	1	2	
12	1	3	2	
13	1	2	3	
14	1	2	3	
15	2	1	3	
16	1	3	2	
17	3	2	1	
18	1	2	3	
19	1	2	3	
20	2	3	1	
21	3	1	2	
22	1	2	3	
23	3	2	1	
24	3	1	2	

Compare your total with the interpretation on the following page.

TOTAL: _____

33

ANGER EXPRESSION QUESTIONNAIRE: Interpretation

Your score shows how strongly each of the following interpretations applies to you as an individual. Most people have a mixture of each of these types, with one being stronger than the others. The closer a score approaches the next category, the more that other category will appear in your personality. For example, if your score is 37, you are generally passive but more assertive than you would be if your score were 29.

If your score is from:

24 to 40   *you are mostly passive.*

41 to 56   *you are mostly assertive.*

57 to 72   *you are mostly aggressive.*

PASSIVE (24 TO 40): You tend to under-react and keep anger inside. You may find that you withdraw from conflict and avoid confrontation. You are probably adaptive, accepting, and patient. You probably suppress strong feelings, especially anger. It may be hard at times to feel happy about anything. Sometimes you feel people take advantage of your good nature.

ASSERTIVE (41 TO 56): You are naturally assertive by nature, or have worked consistently at being open and direct about your feelings. You can express angry feelings with control. You can ask for what you need without guilt. You respect the rights of others when you communicate and can negotiate and problem-solve. You find that people respect you, and feel that you are gentle, yet strong, but not overpowering. You can stand up for yourself without being pushy. You have excellent verbal skills. You tend to be "pro-active"—in other words, you can assess a potential conflict and think of the best way to deal with it before it becomes a crisis.

AGGRESSIVE (57 TO 72): You are more confrontational in your communication. You need to be right or win and may get upset when things don't go your way or when people don't agree with you. You have a strong need to control others and to be in control. You may find it difficult to hear constructive criticism. You may have a tendency to judge other people, but you also have high standards for yourself. People may be intimidated by your style of communication and give in to your requests. You may not be aware of how overbearing you appear, which makes it difficult to change unless you can allow yourself to be vulnerable long enough to hear what people are trying to tell you.

ANGER EXPRESSION QUESTIONNAIRE: Summary

The purpose of this questionnaire was to help you discover how you express your anger and feelings in general. If you found that you tend either to be aggressive or to stuff your anger inside, remember that both behaviors are based on fear, even though they look like polar opposites. Of course, the reasons for fear will be different. Also, both aggressive and passive people may have difficulty recognizing the extent of the anger they feel.

If you want to change your behavior patterns, start by working through concerns. Become aware of physical cues that anger is building and make a decision about what you need to do instead of over-reacting or suppressing your feelings. Watch assertive people and model your behavior after theirs. True assertion is gentle and non-threatening, but also direct and honest. You won't shrivel up if you assert yourself, and you don't need to over-react to make your point. You will learn more about assertive skills in Chapter 10.

I'm not suggesting it will be easy for you to change. Other people may test you at first, making it even more difficult not to give up. Remember, it was you who trained others to respond to you in a certain way. So, it makes sense that it's going to take consistency in the retraining program.

Manipulative people know that shy, unassertive folks will eventually "cave in" to pressure. Being pro-active means that you are already aware of this and will be prepared in advance. Start by practicing being assertive in unthreatening situations or with people who will not react with anger. Remember that we all had to crawl and fall down many times before we walked!

If you want to change your behavior patterns, start by working through concerns.

You will learn more about assertive skills in Chapter 10.

3

The Origins of Anger

NINE

In the Animal Kingdom

As I have indicated previously, we are all born with the ability to feel anger. It is a healthy response to an immediate fear or threat. Well, most animal species also have the innate ability to feel anger. It's part of their survival system, too. I love watching the National Geographic specials. I am especially intrigued by how wild animals use anger to survive. What are they doing when they are angry? I have developed the following story to show how anger is purposeful in the most primal sense, and how animals use anger to set boundaries with each other. Animals can give us great insight into what anger looks like when perfectly mastered.

...we are all born with the ability to feel anger. It is a healthy response to an immediate fear or threat.

The Jungle Story

You are on an African safari and are on the Serengeti Plain. You see a pride of lions lollygagging around under an acacia tree, trying to stay cool in the burning heat of the mid-day sun. All of a sudden, one of them smells an intruder. Another male lion has entered the pride's boundaries, which are invisibly marked by urine.

When a boundary has been breached, the whole pride doesn't jump up and "go for the kill." Usually, one member responds, and don't ask me how they decide that! But one lion will investigate the situation by approaching the intruder. His mere presence may let the intruder know that a boundary has been crossed. The point here is that there are many steps or levels of assessment before an all-out fight occurs. The intruder may wonder off, so that no anger is needed. But let's say that the intruder doesn't get the hint. The other lion might start prancing back and forth, tensing his muscles in an effort to intimidate. He might

39

Boundaries say, "This is mine, and that is yours." They can be emotional or physical. But when they are breached, humans usually get defensive, hurt, or angry.

use grunts or body gestures as a scare tactic. If the intruder still doesn't retreat, the resident lion will probably heighten his anger by growling or running in short bursts toward the outsider. His muscles become tense when he assesses the situation as more threatening. Finally, he has had enough, and starts an all-out chase. The two males may come into physical contact, especially if they are fighting over food, but generally not over a boundary infraction. When the intruder is at a safe distance and is no longer a threat, the lion relaxes and returns to the pride.

This story is a perfect example of anger used effectively. Let's go through the steps and relate it to humans.

- First the lion perceived a threat.

- He then went to investigate. He was assessing the degree of threat.

- Then, the lion made gestures (expressed his feelings) to inform the intruder that indeed there was a problem.

- When the intruder did not pay heed, the lion got physically angry and behaved aggressively. And even then, he didn't kill the intruder (over-react). He used just enough anger to deal with the problem.

If we could use anger the way animals do, we would be able to accurately assess the level of threat, and use just enough anger to deal with the problem, or use no anger at all. Sometimes we over-react automatically, or don't react even when we should. Often we neglect to find out if the threat is to ourselves! If there is indeed a threat, or boundary violation, we should tell others that we have been violated or hurt, and what we need to resolve the problem.

It is fascinating to me that all beings, including animals, need defined boundaries. Boundaries say, "This is mine, and that is yours." They can be emotional or physical. But when they are breached, humans usually get defensive, hurt, or angry. Their responses may be quick and automatic. Unlike animals, people often react before determining the extent of a threat. But since we are intelligent beings with highly sensitized emotions and the ability to reason, we can learn how to manage our world with understanding and skill so that we don't hurt ourselves or others with our behavior.

TEN

In Childhood

Let's start our discussion about the origins of anger in humans from the beginning, birth. We are all born with one well developed behavior—anger. We use it instinctively when we feel hungry, threatened, frightened, lonely, bored, or cold. Anger gives us the feeling that we can influence our world. In other words, we use anger right from birth to get control over our emotional and physical environments. This is illustrated by the following story.

...we use anger right from birth to get control over our emotional and physical environments.

Baby Jane came into the world the same way we all do. She left a warm, cozy "waterbed" and was thrust into a cold open space, dangling by a cord—her lifeline for nine months. Well, she wasn't happy about all that and started to cry angrily. The act of crying actually activated her sympathetic nervous system, thus giving her life. Adrenaline started flowing and her lungs filled up with air. She was really angry, and full of life!

The anger reaction (crying) calls a caregiver to the baby's side. Now, baby Jane does not know all this. She just wants to be fed, warmed, and comforted. But in a very short time, she begins to put the pieces together. She figures out that crying (getting angry) is a powerful tool for getting what she wants. Unconsciously, she stores this behavior in her mind as "need-fulfilling." She has begun to learn how to control her environment.

If baby Jane has responsive parents, she doesn't have to cry all the time in order to have her needs met. She learns that if she acts frustrated (a lesser form of all-out anger), her mom or dad will try to figure out what she needs. If she has inexperienced or unresponsive parents, she quickly learns that she must get really angry before someone will respond. If nobody comes most of the time, even when she is screaming angry, she will give up trying to influence her world.

Jane is also learning other behaviors, such as smiling, which attract her caregivers' attention. So she "files" smiling in her mind as another need-fulfilling behavior. But what happens if Jane smiles when she's hungry? Do you think she'll get food? No. Baby Jane quickly realizes that she must use some level of anger if she wants to be fed.

Babies learn hundreds of behaviors and by trial and error figure out what behavior works best under what circumstance. We all want control of our world and, like baby Jane, will choose what we feel is the most effective behavior at the time.

Many years ago, when I supervised a Mother-Child Residence for young mothers and their infants, I witnessed profound examples of what happens to babies who do not get enough attention. When babies "signal" their needs and meet with no reaction from their caregivers, they often become unresponsive after just a few months. The babies I worked with would not try to get my attention by crying or smiling. They just sat there, often mentally slow and even physically underdeveloped. I talked to these babies, held them, and tried to get them to mimic my facial expressions, but so often, their condition was irreversible. I found that the extent of the damage depended on the age of the baby and how profound the neglect was. The lack of sufficient loving attention and warm, trusting relationships has been medically proven to result in mental retardation due to the lack of bonding, which must occur in the early months of life (Clayman, p. 399).

While feelings are innate, the expression of feelings is learned in families—we either imitate or reject what we learn.

feelings
↓
innate
(instinctive)

expression
↓
learned
(in families)

The spoken and unspoken rules we grow up by influence our feelings and our behavior as adults. What happens if we grow up in an environment where people believe that in ideal family relationships there should be no conflict or anger? Anger under these circumstances is camouflaged by denial, and we learn ways to dodge conflict by avoiding, lying, hiding, or trying to cheer everyone up, or by getting good grades or being the "perfect" child. The unspoken anger comes out only when it can no longer be kept inside, and by then it has become rage. Alas, this well-learned pattern for avoiding conflict is often carried into adulthood. A child who has stuffed anger may become an enraged adult, finally able to fight back. You may have heard a parent say, "I don't what know what happened to my son. He was such a good boy, and now he's turned into a defiant teenager. His grades are terrible and he won't listen to us anymore."

Conversely, anger may be expressed in extreme ways, such as physical or emotional abuse. This is especially true in dysfunctional or alcoholic family systems. Anger is used as a "weapon" for manipulation, or not used consistently, thus confusing the child about what the "rules" are. The child becomes so afraid of anger that he or she has no choice but to run from it, or to fight back with more anger. Angry children often become angry adults.

I have discovered through counseling teens and adults that it is not atypical for one parent to be overt (over-reacting) in expressing anger, while the other parent compensates by under-reacting and minimizing or denying the extent of anger in the house.

Children growing up in these difficult family environments live in anger where nothing is resolved. If children feel threatened, see anger, and feel anger, but someone tells them, "Don't get angry," their sense of what is "real" is distorted and denied. In other words, what they see, hear, and feel is in conflict with what they are being told or shown.

Thus, as adults, many of us are still afraid of our own anger and that of others. In an effort to keep this frightening emotion at a safe distance, we begin not to trust what we see, hear, and feel. We may find it very difficult after a while to determine what we're feeling. So when any uncomfortable emotion arises, we may numb it out completely or rationalize it to make us feel safer.

I believe that most parents do the best that they can, given their own upbringing (the lessons they were taught); their current lifestyle (addiction may consume them and be more important than parenting); their parenting skills and discipline techniques; and a host of other variables. I am not saying, however, that these factors are good excuses for poor parenting, for allowing a child to grow up neglected or abused. It is sad that all children cannot have all the love, attention, and care that each and every one of us deserves.

Children also do the best they can, given the environments they are in. Children are survivors and extremely resilient. Despite abuse and neglect, they can grow into loving adults who can learn new, healthy ways of interacting with others.

The following story is about a boy who learned many lessons from his father while he was growing up.

THE BRICK MAN STORY*

Once upon a time on a far-away island lived a boy and his father. When the boy was very young, his father gave him a sack and said to him, "This sack is very important. When I am angry with you, or discouraged, or unhappy with you, I will throw a brick at you. You are to put the brick in your sack and carry it around to remind yourself of how mad I am at you, and how you made me mad, or sad, or frustrated, or discouraged."

The boy's father threw a lot of bricks, as he was a very talented brick thrower. The little boy gathered all these bricks and put them in his sack. The sack became heavier and heavier.

As the boy grew up, it became increasingly difficult to carry around the sack of bricks, even though his father continued to throw them at him and the boy continued to put them in his sack. By the time the boy became a man, it was so hard to carry his sack of bricks that it was almost impossible for him to go anywhere.

He heard of a magic island where someone would help relieve him of his load. So he took the sack with the bricks and struggled to a boat. When he reached the magic island, he hauled his sack of bricks to the magician's hut.

44

* From Bev Carle, "The Boat People" (unpublished story, Edmonton, Alberta, 1986). Adapted with permission of the author.

He said, "I don't know what to do. I can't go anywhere with my sack of bricks—I can't do anything. What should I do?"

The magician replied, "I can do nothing with your bricks. You must think of what to do so you can begin to move."

So the man thought and thought and thought, and finally he realized that it had been his own choice to put the bricks in the sack. So he went through all the bricks in his sack to learn what he needed to learn. He figured out new skills and beliefs so he wouldn't ever again collect bricks from his father or anyone else.

And after he did that, he took his sack with the bricks and he went to the highest cliff on the island and threw his sack of bricks into the ocean.

EXERCISE

Write down what you think this story means. Why would a father throw bricks at his son? What "messages" were on each brick? What does it mean that his son threw the bricks into the ocean?

_____

_____

_____

_____

_____

_____

_____

_____

_____

_____

_____

_____

_____

_____

_____

_____

_____

Personalize "The Brick Man Story" and relate it to your own experiences as a child and young man or woman.

_____

_____

_____

_____

_____

_____

_____

_____

_____

_____

_____

_____

_____

_____

_____

DEVELOPING AN ANGER METAPHOR

In order to help you personalize your own anger experience, try the following exercise. Draw a picture of your anger. You can use words or symbols if you like. Use the next page, or a larger piece of paper. Get some colored markers, or borrow your child's crayons. Some people find it helpful to close their eyes and just start drawing whatever comes to mind. There is no wrong picture! Have fun!

If you want, you can share your picture with someone you trust. Feedback from a close friend or relative might help you to get a different perspective on your anger.

A Picture of My Anger

ELEVEN

What Do I Feel?

If you're not ready to acknowledge your anger, it builds up inside, until there's such an overload that it seeps out...or explodes in rage.

The rules we grew up with influence our feelings and behavior. What did you discover from your picture about your anger? For many years, you may not have been able to trust your anger or other feelings. Do you find that you don't know what you feel, or who you really are? Many people I have worked with say this is so for them. When they don't allow themselves to express anger at the person they are angry with, their unconscious mind becomes exhausted, because it feels all feelings. The unconscious mind is the wise part that knows the truth. We only become consciously aware of the truth when we're safe and ready. If you're not ready to acknowledge your anger, it builds up inside, until there's such an overload that it seeps out, often inappropriately, or explodes in rage.

SELF-HELP QUESTIONS: Childhood Learning

Answer the following questions to gain insight into your childhood.

1. Who in your past expressed anger outwardly?

2. Who in your past turned anger inward, although you felt it nevertheless?

3. As a child, how were you influenced by the anger expression of important people in your life?

In order to get to know your feelings better, and ultimately be able to handle your anger more appropriately, fill in the following picture. Fill in the outer part of "you" first, starting clockwise at the top. Then fill in the inner part of "you." This exercise may take some time and thought. It's not easy to think about feelings and needs that you may have buried for many years.

My Feelings

I see in my future:

_____

_____

_____

_____

_____

I need:

_____

_____

_____

_____

_____

I would describe me this way:

1. _____
2. _____
3. _____
4. _____
5. _____
6. _____
7. _____
8. _____
9. _____

I feel happy when:

_____

_____

_____

_____

_____

I feel angry when:

_____

_____

_____

_____

_____

Right now I feel:

_____

_____

_____

_____

People who respect me are:

_____

_____

_____

_____

I am afraid of:

_____

_____

_____

_____

TWELVE

How to Heal an Unhealthy Childhood

The ideal response is to talk about anger when it surfaces, learn where it comes from, and decide how not to repeat it.

If we don't choose to let go of a past that continues to erode our self-esteem and interfere with our ability to enjoy healthy relationships, then we are truly the captives of our past. People who are still hurting usually experience fear—fear of not being loved, fear of being abandoned, fear of making a mistake, fear of being a mistake, and fear of not getting what they want and need now because they didn't have those needs met in childhood.

A healthy way to deal with not getting what we wanted is to mourn, get angry, accept, and move on to create a new life filled with all those things we need. It's an important part of healing to go back and acknowledge the pain as part of the grieving process. This helps us to get in touch with our feelings.

Those who continue to blame without letting go will stay fixated at the point of their pain and often feel and act like victims. Many of them will turn to compulsive behaviors as a way to escape the pain, but this only increases the pain tenfold. The ideal response is to talk about anger when it surfaces, learn where it comes from, and decide how not to repeat it. We do react according to our history. If we don't resolve childhood anger, we punish ourselves and others.

People who are hurting tend to hurt other people.

STRATEGIES FOR HEALING YOUR PAST

1. Increase your awareness of your anger issues.

The first step in exploring your anger issues is to ask yourself about your childhood experiences. Was there a hidden rule that said, "Do not express your anger," or "What you hear, see, and feel is not real"? Are you holding on to your anger as a defense against some painful feelings and issues that lie beneath it? For some, choosing anger is less threatening than risking vulnerability. Remember, if we don't resolve anger, we punish.

How do you express your anger now?

2. Take responsibility for your behavior.

Regardless of your childhood experience, you choose your anger responses as an adult. Sometimes as adults we forget that we have the power to change old beliefs. We can move out of a "victim" stance by communicating needs directly and assertively. If we don't see that it is our responsibility to ensure our own happiness, we become blamers, and nothing will ever change.

What can you change about your current anger expression that would make a positive difference?

3. Forgive.

The purpose of looking at childhood influences is not to blame our past, but to increase our awareness of anger so that we can understand what causes it. If you cannot forgive those responsible for even the most difficult childhood experiences, you will be an angry adult—defensive, punishing, blaming. If you did not get what you needed as a child, make sure you take care of your own emotional needs now, without assuming that other people should be responsible for them. Forgiveness nourishes the soul and makes room for loving relationships.

Who do you need to forgive, so you can move on to a happier life? (You may want to include yourself.)

THIRTEEN

How Do I Know I'm Loved?

We all experience the world from different points of view.

Most people I talk with as a counselor say their childhood was unhappy, or dysfunctional in some aspect. How people describe their childhood is so diverse, ranging from extremely neglectful and abusive to quite loving and close. Children from the same family can have very different experiences. Again, it's our perception that shapes our perspective. While it's unrealistic to think that we can get all of our needs met all of the time, it's important, in my experience, to have had caregivers who showed you love in a way that you could recognize, and to have received at least some of what you needed the most.

Let me expand on the notion of the importance of receiving love in a way that you could recognize. We all experience the world from different points of view. Some people know they are cared for when they hear the words "I love you," or some other expression of affection. Other people need to see the caring in action—in other words, they know they're cared for when the other person does nice things. A third group of people need to feel love through physical touch. As an example, let's go back to visit Mary and John Doe.

THE CASE OF MARY AND JOHN DOE: PART 2

Mary grew up needing to hear loving words in order to be sure she was cared for. She also enjoyed feeling love and physical contact, but hearing those three little words, "I love you," really meant everything to her. She didn't need John to do things for her, such as bringing flowers or taking her out for dinner, which he often did. Those things were nice, but third on her list nonetheless.

John, on the other hand, grew up learning that if you love someone, you should not have to say so. In fact, he was taught that "actions speak louder than words," so he always did things for Mary. He wasn't comfortable with "gushy" talk, and physical demonstrations of affection were reserved for the privacy of the bedroom.

Well, we can see that these two are not connecting in the ways they show they care and know they're cared for. Mary perceives that John does not love her because he never says so. She thinks that he just placates her by taking her out to dinner often. John thinks everything is fine because Mary does lots of things for him, such as cooking wonderful meals, ironing his shirts, and cleaning the house.

A person's childhood doesn't have to be riddled with abuse and neglect in order for a child to feel unloved.

The following chart demonstrates how Mary's first choice of how she knows she is cared for is exactly opposite to John's preferred method of showing that he cares. These dynamics are quite common. Perhaps that's why we coin the phrase "opposites attract."

How Do They Know They Are Loved?

Mary	John
1. Hear loving words	1. Do loving things
2. Feel (touch)	2. Feel (touch)
3. Do loving things	3. Hear loving words

We can visualize how this couple faces a problem I hear about so often: two people love each other, but neither one recognizes that he or she is loved!

This same scenario often takes place in childhood as well. A child may grow up feeling unloved because the same "system" for caring wasn't being applied. A person's childhood doesn't have to be riddled with abuse and neglect in order for a child to feel unloved. It's not a case where one method of showing you care is "the right way," it's a compatibility problem. A mother may feel closer to one child because that child uses the same system for caring. So, in all this, there may be an important lesson: you may need to "reframe," or look at your childhood experience from a different perspective.

4

Why Do We "Choose" Anger Behavior?

FOURTEEN

Long-Term Feelings of Anger

Why do we choose anger if we dislike it so much? Part of the answer lies in the fact that we don't have a choice in the initial, often intense, feeling of anger. This is because anger is innate. We're born with the ability to feel anger. It is a biological process that automatically happens in the brain as a response to stress, excitement, or threat. For example, if someone has just smashed into your car, your immediate response will probably be intense anger at the other driver. This is a healthy, normal reaction. You could have been injured, your car is wrecked, and you're probably in mild shock. We do choose, however, our long-term feelings—in other words, how we feel and what we do after the initial event. What we actually do is to choose our long-term behaviors (loving, being angry, or being depressed) as a way of dealing with the initial feeling.

It is true that people can push our buttons, or trigger an anger response, but no one can make us choose to stay angry.

Many people conclude that our feelings "happen to us." So many times I've been told, "People make me angry!" It is true that people can push our buttons, or trigger an anger response, but no one can make us choose to stay angry.

Following is a partial list of why we might choose long-term feelings of anger:

- Out of habit. The behavior of anger expression is learned in childhood. It can become so automatic a response that we often don't even know when we are "angering" until after the fact.

- To get what we want. We will choose any behavior that helps us get our physical and/or emotional needs met. If I think that by getting angry, or raising my voice, I will make someone respond to my wishes, then I will use anger. Like any other emo-

57

tion or behavior, anger can be need-fulfilling. It can be used to gain attention or power.

- To get others to help us. "Angering" is a powerful behavior that can invoke a response from others. The anger can be subtle, turned inward to look like helplessness. People often fall into the trap of "enabling" (doing for others what they can, or should, do for themselves) when this type of anger is used. It is the subtle anger that hooks us in most often.

- To excuse not taking responsibility for choosing more effective behaviors. For example, many parents continue to yell or hit their children, even after they take a parenting course, instead of using "time-out" discipline or some other approach that takes more time and practice.

- To gain control. Let's face it, we all like to feel in control at times. Some people have more of that need, and will use anger to intimidate or manipulate others. In other words, anger is used to "win," or be "right."

- To hide other feelings. Many people, especially men, find it more acceptable to be angry than to let hurt, pain, or sadness show (Campbell, p. 42). Women more often internalize their anger, or "cry it out" in a effort to release frustration and other feelings without causing physical injury (Campbell, p. 45).

- Because we assume the situation is dangerous. We may have had a similar experience in the past which did cause harm, or we may perceive that we don't have the skills to handle the event. Sometimes not knowing why the situation is threatening can be threatening! For example, I may get angry at my child for not getting good grades in school. I may not realize that the threat is actually to my perception of myself as a good parent. I may think that poor grades = poor parenting. I may project my anger on the child, instead of realizing that my own insecurity is the problem. Often, diagnosing the perceived threat reveals that it is simply the result of a difference in values, opinions, upbringing, or styles of behaving.

FIFTEEN

When Is Anger a Healthy Choice?

Remember, anger is a signal that we need to pay attention to something, emotionally or physically. In other words, anger is our natural "boundary setter." The signal we get lets us know when a personal boundary has been crossed.

You can use the anger as a motivator to do something...

Examples of some boundary violations:

- When we need to defend ourselves in a threatening situation, such as physical, sexual, or emotional abuse.

- When a life-threatening situation endangers us or someone we love.

- When someone is manipulating or intimidating us.

Examples of healthy uses of anger feelings or expression:

- When the energy from anger is a motivator for positive change.

- When anger helps us move through the grieving process or loss. Anger is one of many defense mechanisms that allow us to react to an emotionally devastating experience without falling apart. It gives us time to deal with the situation. We will discuss this topic more fully in the next few pages.

- When the anger "energy" enables us to assert ourselves and express feelings openly.

- When anger enables us to react to a threat. For example, if your child runs out into traffic, the anger response provides adrenaline so you can act quickly, without fear.

Anger can be a constructive response to almost all internal or external events that cause hurt, frustration, or fear. For example, when someone has criticized you, you feel hurt and angry. You can use the anger as a motivator to do something, so that the inner pain is minimized and you don't become paralyzed by your feelings.

59

SIXTEEN

How Much Anger Is Okay?

Many people believe that anger is a bad feeling, to be avoided and not displayed at all. That is denying anger. We often try to locate the source of anger outside of ourselves by blaming someone else ("You make me angry," or "You bother me."). However, anger is interpersonal, between people. We allow ourselves to become angry.

You might feel that there are no degrees of anger. You're either angry or you're not. Part of dealing with anger is becoming aware of the differences in its intensity. For some people, learning to get a *little* angry may help to change the "all or nothing" concept. Does the intensity of your anger vary according to the situation, or do you tend to give every incident a "10"?

Anger Expression Scale

Repressed anger	Some awareness	Denies own anger	Angry at self	Healthy expression	Annoyed, frustrated	Tense, stressed	Very angry	Verbal rage	Physically Abusive
1	2	3	4	5	6	7	8	9	10

Mark where you would rate your present level of anger on most days.

You can't fight all battles in life. Choose what is important, and let the rest go. Sometimes people don't realize they are still fighting a battle that has been over for years. A good example is unresolved childhood issues. If you are an adult, you can make new choices about your relationships. You are not a child anymore, and can set healthy boundaries with family members so you don't remain a victim. So many clients have told me, "I've always fought with my parents, that's just the way it is. They'll never change." My response is, "Then you teach them how you want to be treated."

EXERCISE: Myths about Anger

Myth 1: An effective way to release anger is to punch a punching bag or get involved in any other strenuous exercise.

How do you release your anger? Are you able to address the feelings and try to resolve the issues? If not, what stops you?

Reality: Strenuous exercise only tires the muscles. Relieving anger energy by going for a walk or to the gym to "cool down" instead of becoming violent is healthy only if you also address the reason for the angry feelings. Otherwise, the anger will surface again and again. When anger surfaces, allow yourself to feel what's behind the anger. Remember, anger is a signal that lets us know we are threatened.

Myth 2: If you express anger in a relationship, it will jeopardize the intimacy and you run the risk of being abandoned.

Do you believe that expressing anger will destroy relationships or friendships? From whom or where did you learn this?

_____

_____

_____

Reality: A lot of people try to protect relationships by not making waves, but unspoken feelings only deepen the hurt and fear. It is healthy to own your anger and share it openly. Using "I" statements decreases the urge to blame the other person for your feelings. Sharing your feelings provides an opportunity for the other person to clarify her or his position, and can make the relationship closer. However, expressing anger will damage a friendship if it is based on the unspoken premise that in an ideal relationship there should be no anger.

Myth 3: Some people never seem to get angry.

Have you heard this statement from others? Do you agree?

_____

_____

_____

Reality: Everyone has angry feelings from time to time. Some people try to repress any hint of anger in order to look and sound "nice" or "in control." They have to work pretty hard at times to stuff unpleasant feelings, but usually the anger bursts out in a verbally or physically aggressive manner, surprising everyone. People tend to suppress anger when they don't know how to ask for what they need or when they are unable to say no to a request.

Myth 4: Yelling, hitting, or throwing things is understandable when someone makes you angry.

Have you ever used any form of physical aggression when you are angry? Do you believe that others can make you angry? If so, explain why.

_____

_____

_____

Reality: Firstly, violence of any type cannot be justified, unless, of course, you are fighting for your life. Secondly, no one can "make" you angry. We choose our feelings. If you give your personal power away by allowing others to govern your state of mind through their words and actions, you will most certainly be more defensive and out of control.

Myth 5: Anger is unhealthy.

Do you believe it is unhealthy to feel angry? Why or why not?

_____

_____

_____

Reality: Having angry feelings is normal. It's what we do with our angry feelings that can present a problem. For example, anger that is channeled into hostility or aggression can damage ourselves or others. Hostility is a negative attitude that results from a sense of powerlessness and an inability to assert oneself. Aggression, on the other hand, is a behavior, one of the more visible forms of anger.

People who are unable to recognize anger in their lives may feel that they have been hurt too many times in the past. Many misconceptions and assumptions about anger stem from a distrust, and even denial, of our emotions. It may be too painful to acknowledge the anger. However, our feelings, including anger, help us to evaluate our actions, and give us an opportunity to know ourselves better. When we are in touch with our feelings, we are best able to be in control of ourselves, and less reactive.

The following chapter will help you to evaluate personal and environmental factors that may provoke the anger response in you.

5

Factors That Can Trigger the Anger Response

SEVENTEEN

Personal Factors

In my experience, it's our **needs** that drive our feelings and behaviors the most. When I speak of needs, I am not referring to the need to have food, water, and housing; I'm referring to emotional needs. Examples of some basic emotional needs are the need for love and approval, the need for self-respect, the need to have fun, the need for the freedom to make choices. Our needs are different from our wants, in that needs are much more powerful. Wants are desires; we won't suffer greatly if we don't get what we want. Our needs are more basic; we are almost unconsciously driven to fulfill these needs. Even someone who is in jail may find a way to have some fun, make choices, get internal power (self-esteem), and find companionship. Human beings are very adaptable.

...our values shape the way we treat people, and how we feel about the world in general.

Other factors that influence our behavior are our **values**. For example, I value the dignity and worth of individuals. Therefore, I try to treat everyone with respect. You may value something entirely different. The important thing to note is that our values shape the way we treat people, and how we feel about the world in general.

Assumptions are beliefs we take for granted, whether they are true or not. They can be very unhelpful when we're trying to change unhealthy anger patterns. If you assume incorrectly that someone will respond in a certain way because other people have done so in the past, you may react inappropriately instead of responding to the circumstances of each situation.

Our **past experience** also shapes our feelings and behaviors, as we saw in the chapter on childhood learnings. Previous experience sometimes keeps us in fear. Fear is a strong, unpleasant emotion, usually caused by the anticipation or awareness of some danger, real or imagined. Fear can paralyze us in the face

67

of danger, or we can react aggressively. It's difficult to "rewrite" the future if your past is still affecting you in a negative way.

Included in our past experience is our **cultural upbringing**, that is, the norms of the society we grew up in. These customary beliefs influence our behavior and perceptions of the world.

One issue that seems to be significant for the people I have worked with involves **authority figures**. Many individuals feel they are under the power and control of people in authority, and find themselves unable to respond assertively. Some people report that they revert back to childhood, in that they feel intimidated and "lose their voice."

EIGHTEEN

Environmental Factors

Environmental factors can also influence our anger response. Our surroundings, including our place of employment, can have a tremendous impact on our feelings and behavior. Many people say they have less control in public environments, where they feel more vulnerable. Therefore, anger in the workplace is often "displaced," or expressed in a safer environment, such as at home.

Our surroundings, including our place of employment, can have a tremendous impact on our feelings and behavior.

Let's explore work and stress, which often result in internalized anger. There seems to be a significant relationship between stressful external factors and physical illness and injury on the job. The reasons are multi-faceted, and can include factors such as the stress associated with working in the helping professions; low pay; boring or repetitive work; work overload; lack of control over decisions or conditions; rapid change (which is certainly an issue these days!); fear or anticipation of job loss; continual crises; long hours; isolation from colleagues, friends, or family; negative interpersonal relationships with other employees; lack of trust; lack of clear communication; not feeling appreciated or valued; and general job dissatisfaction. That's quite some list.

The relationship between stress and illness or injury applies to other major areas of life, such as our home, social, and educational environments. Whenever we are in a situation in which we must relate to or interact with others, we become more vulnerable. In other words, our environments can shape our behavior (Campbell, p. 10).

Expressing anger is a way of letting go of frustration and stress caused by environmental factors. The body, as indicated earlier, "revs up" in response to stress by

69

...when we face intense stress, our bodies release chemicals to restore balance. When the stress is constant due to environmental conditions we cannot control, our emotions and bodies eventually "burn out."

releasing certain hormones. These chemicals are strong inhibitors of the immune system and are not meant to work continually at high levels. In other words, the chemicals are released in order to help the body handle short-term crises. The immune system as a whole is weakened when the body is under constant stress. I like to use the analogy of what happens when we injure ourselves physically to illustrate this process.

Let's say you gash your hand. Your body immediately sends in white blood cells to help coagulate the blood and speed the healing process. But the body's immune system is temporarily weakened until the white blood count is restored to equilibrium. The larger the injury, the more susceptible you are to infection or the weakening of other organs.

Well, when we face intense stress, our bodies release chemicals to restore balance. When the stress is constant due to environmental conditions we cannot control, our emotions and bodies eventually "burn out."

Ask yourself if any conditions in your environments are contributing to your anger and threatening your physical health and emotional well-being. We will be talking about personal self-care and prevention strategies later in the book, but perhaps there is one small thing that you could change now that would make a big difference.

SELF-HELP WORKSHEET: When Do Your Buttons Get Pushed?

Identify your anger triggers in items 1 to 3. Give examples and explain why these are your triggers. Then reflect on these lists as you answer questions 4 to 12.

1. Certain people (authority figures; men or women in general; their tone of voice, size, behavior)

2. Certain events (such traffic, family or social gatherings, meetings)

3. Emotional and physical states (such as fatigue, hunger, stress, deprivation)

4. Are you aware of what makes you angry, or do you react without understanding what your feelings are? Describe a recent incident and try to analyze what you were feeling that triggered the anger response.

5. Are you currently grieving a recent loss (such as a relationship or job), or a loss in the past (such as an unhappy childhood)? If so, describe how you are expressing your grief.

6. Do you get angry at yourself? If so, why?

7. Do you get hooked into other people's anger? If so, describe the circumstances when this happens.

8. If you have children, is there something they do (or don't do) that triggers your anger? Why?

9. What do others do to push your buttons?

10. Do you use your anger to get a reaction from others? If so, how?

11. What triggers your anger on the job? (Consider the discussion at the beginning of this section.)

12. Review your previous responses. What in your life is most likely to trigger your anger?

6

Anger and the Grieving Process

NINETEEN

The Five Stages of Loss

Elisabeth Kübler-Ross, who spent many years caring for people with terminal illnesses, identified five "stages" that her patients seemed to experience: denial, anger, bargaining, depression, and acceptance. Not all people go through all stages in the same order or in the same amount of time. Let's look at the stages individually.

Anger comes when we no longer feel in control of a situation, such as the death of a loved one, or our own ill health.

1. **Denial.** This is a healthy defense mechanism that allows us to temporarily reject a painful reality until we can deal with the shock.

2. **Anger.** When the reality of the loss sets in, denial is replaced by anger. Blame or displaced anger is often directed at other people. Anger comes when we no longer feel in control of a situation, such as the death of a loved one, or our own ill health.

3. **Bargaining.** We try to make an "agreement" in the hope of postponing the inevitable. Most bargains are attempted with God and are often kept secret.

4. **Depression.** A great sense of sadness can prepare us for various types of loss.

5. **Acceptance.** If we have time, we may be able to express our feelings and mourn the loss. Acceptance does not mean we are happy, but we realize the struggle is over. When we don't accept and mourn a loss, we can become fixated at the point of pain. In other words, we focus on the pain and find it extremely difficult to let go.

Types of Loss Associated with the Grieving Process

Obvious	Less Obvious	Everyday
death	illness (loss of good health)	broken promise
rape	loss of success	dent in car
divorce	giving up an addiction	missed phone call
loss of child	loss of self-esteem, status	disappointment
moving, loss of home	marriage breakdown	
loss of job	friction between friends	
abortion	incarceration (loss of freedom)	

Make a list of the losses in your life, both recent and past. Do these losses play a role in your anger?

Obvious	Less Obvious	Everyday

_____

_____

_____

_____

_____

_____

_____

_____

_____

_____

_____

After reviewing your lists, put a star beside the losses that are still significant today.

TWENTY

Depression as "Frozen Anger"

The purpose of anger is to prepare us to protect our emotional and physical well-being, particularly in situations that cause us to feel hurt, frustrated, or fearful. When we are faced with a loss, a common way to hang on to what we don't want to let go of is to remain angry. The anger is a purposeful defense in that it gives us energy to fight emotionally, to deal with the pain in our own time. If we hang on to the anger for too long, however, it becomes "stuck," or "frozen," and we become depressed.

Long-term depression could be seen as an inability to use the power made available through the arousal of anger.

Depression is caused by chemical changes in the brain. If we experience a prolonged sense of powerlessness, or if an event suddenly produces feelings of helplessness or intense sadness, our brains respond by altering the amount of certain neurotransmitters. These chemicals are responsible for our mood, thought processes, and eating and sleeping habits. When the brain slows down the production of these chemicals, which could be thought of as "brain food," we slow down as well. We need proper levels of these chemicals in order to think clearly and maintain our emotional balance.

When depression is prolonged, we often respond by feeling inadequate, and may focus obsessively on our failings or loss. The end result is that we can reduce our self-esteem to dangerous, sometimes suicidal, levels. Long-term depression could be seen as an inability to use the power made available through the arousal of anger. Depressed people, including those who are potentially suicidal, are expressing anger inward. Some people describe depression as "frozen anger" because it is locked inside. In therapy, I might try to help depressed people get in touch with their anger in order to move through the grieving process.

Let's face it, we all have periods when we feel worthless, afraid, useless, or alone. Events such as death, divorce, or the loss of a job can trigger a depressed mood. Sometimes short-term depression may actually help us to avoid hasty, angry behaviors that may make a situation worse. This is normal. When the depression lasts a long time, however, or prevents you from being yourself, you should seek professional help

77

7

Anger and Addictions

TWENTY-ONE

Addictions and Unresolved Anger

Anger is a natural process that lets us know when we are feeling emotionally threatened. Long-term, unresolved anger is often related to hurt or loss. If we don't believe that we have the power or the skills to deal with the issue, we might get addicted to those behaviors that help stuff the pain and keep anger at bay. For instance, let's say that you have an overpowering boss who daily pushes your buttons. You have never been assertive by nature, and feel that confronting your employer will probably only make things worse. So, to relieve the tension and divert your angry feelings, you (unconsciously) start compulsively eating, gambling, drinking, taking drugs, smoking cigarettes, or being sexually promiscuous. These behaviors act as a release valve. If you can't control one area of your life, you can certainly put a glass to your mouth.

Long-term, unresolved anger is often related to hurt or loss.

But dealing with stuffed anger through these eventually self-destructive behaviors does not do anything to change the circumstances. Numbing anger through addictive behaviors does not effectively keep problems or pain away—it only deepens the pain, giving it power. People often tell me that the added guilt of the addiction only compounds the problem. They still have the original upsetting event, plus now they have behaviors that they cannot control.

Anger seems to be the one emotion that is common in the lives of addicts and recovering addicts. Many people acknowledge that they use alcohol or drugs to numb angry feelings or, conversely, to enable them to express bottled-up emotions. Either way, their anger is not managed well, resulting in shame, guilt, and remorse for past behavior. The fear and avoidance of anger create much anxiety.

As you read this section, see if you can pinpoint some behavior patterns that may be leading to an unbalanced lifestyle, including an addiction to a substance or behavior (including anger). Some people are "addicted" to the power rush from an outburst of anger.

TWENTY-TWO

Self-Assessment of a Potential Addiction Problem

Addictions and other compulsions may be signs of unresolved anger. Of course, other reasons such as mental illness cannot be overlooked. For our purposes, though, we will focus only on the relationship between anger and addictions.

It has been my experience that most people who enter into treatment have problems with anger—either anger turned inward or anger expressed outwardly. A few individuals may not recognize an anger-addiction problem initially, but say they are depressed, or that they "blow-up" periodically.

DEFINITION OF ADDICTION

An addiction can be defined as any compulsive behavior such as drinking, eating, taking mood-altering drugs, or sexual promiscuity that cannot easily be stopped, even though the behavior has a detrimental effect on a person's life.

Let's explore the differences between use, mis-use, and abuse, with the consumption of drugs as an example. Use could be defined as taking a drug as prescribed, and not for the purpose of altering one's mood. Mis-use occurs when a drug is taken more often than prescribed, or has been obtained without a prescription, and is used occasionally to alter one's mood. Abuse occurs when a legal or illegal drug is taken specifically for its mood-altering effects. Drug abusers may be unable to stop taking the drug, even though they want to; if they do stop, they may experience withdrawal symptoms.

There is also a difference between physical addiction—when a person's body needs a substance to maintain the drug levels it is accustomed to and requires in order to prevent withdrawal symptoms, and psychological addiction—when a person craves the drug, but may have no evident signs of physical addiction.

Why do we choose behaviors that have negative effects on our emotional and physical well-being? All behaviors we choose are "need-fulfilling." We don't choose behaviors for no reason at all, unless, of course, we have a personality dysfunction. We often get addicted to those behaviors that we believe will make us happier or keep us safe from emotional pain. For instance, a person who is feeling lonely or bored might start drinking in a bar. A person who is grieving after the death of a loved one or an abusive childhood might start compulsively eating or drinking to numb the pain.

Many substance abusers deny having problems because there is no apparent physical dependency, or they've never gotten into legal trouble. This indicates that they are either in the early process of addiction or they have been lucky, so far.

We often get addicted to those behaviors that we believe will make us happier or keep us safe from emotional pain.

SELF-HELP QUESTIONS

The following questions may help you determine if your current substance use or behavior is a problem.

1. What is your current method of expressing anger?

2. Is there a connection between anger and any substance you are currently choosing? Do you use to control or express anger? If so, give an example.

3. Do you have frequent outbursts of anger that, when combined with substance use, have resulted in involvement with the law? If so, give an example.

4. How did your family of origin deal with anger? Was any addictive behavior apparent?

5. Who makes you the most angry? Do you get revenge by abusing drugs or alcohol and confronting the person, or do you use to stop yourself from acting out your revenge fantasies?

6. If you have been involved with the law as a result of your anger, were you intoxicated or high when most of the offenses occurred?

7. Is there a medical factor that might predispose you to use when you are angry (for example, a history of mental illness, including severe depression)?

8. What effects have your substance abuse and anger had on family, friends, and co-workers?

9. Have you ever attempted to control an addiction? If so, what did you do? How successful were your efforts?

10. Do you think you have an addiction problem now?

IS MY SUBSTANCE USE A PROBLEM?

Answer the following questions to help determine if your drug or alcohol use is a problem for you or others.

	1 never	2 at times	3 often	4 usually	5 always
1. Do I use to control negative feelings?	_____	_____	_____	_____	_____
2. Do I use to celebrate when I'm in a good mood?	_____	_____	_____	_____	_____
3. Do I generally use on the weekends?	_____	_____	_____	_____	_____
4. Have I ever felt bad or ashamed after using?	_____	_____	_____	_____	_____
5. Do I use when I get angry?	_____	_____	_____	_____	_____
6. Do I use to alter my mood?	_____	_____	_____	_____	_____
7. Have I ever done things I normally wouldn't do to get drugs or alcohol (stealing, prostitution)?	_____	_____	_____	_____	_____
8. Have other people ever been concerned about my use (family, friends, Child Welfare)?	_____	_____	_____	_____	_____
9. Can I stop when I want to, or when I say I will?	_____	_____	_____	_____	_____
10. Has my use affected my children, family, or friends?	_____	_____	_____	_____	_____
11. Do I ever wonder if I should quit for good?	_____	_____	_____	_____	_____

WHERE AM I IN THE PROCESS OF DEPENDENCY?

Assess where you are by putting an X on the line, using the following scale:

Use occasionally, social use only, medical use as prescribed	Use more than intended, to feel better or numb feelings, can't always stop	Drug-seeking, have neglected responsibilities, usually can't stop
USE	**MIS-USE**	**ABUSE**

Give examples of your alcohol or other drug use pattern and describe how it is related to your anger.

_____

_____

_____

_____

_____

_____

_____

_____

_____

_____

_____

_____

After looking at my answers, do I think I should cut down?_____

stop altogether? _____

go for assessment? _____

DETOXIFICATION, WITHDRAWAL, AND ANGER

Anger is a predictable part of detoxification, and learning to cope with it can positively influence long-term abstinence.

If you have determined that you do have an addiction problem, and have decided to try to stop your substance abuse, you may find that during the initial withdrawal and detoxification stages, you will experience negative physical and emotional effects to varying degrees, depending on the substance, amount, and length of abuse. The body goes through physical withdrawal, resulting in sickness and pain. The central nervous system works hard to restore balance. Negative emotions, such as depression and anger, are usually strong immediately after detoxification.

Powell and Taylor discovered that while anxiety and depression subsided, anger remained strong. Even after five weeks of in-patient treatment and support, people reported discomforting levels of anger. That's to be expected; they are giving up a substance that has met strong needs in the past. But because the anger is so intense, it tends to increase the risk that they will leave treatment and relapse. Specific interventions are necessary to help people to manage their anger. One useful tip is to expect this initial anger and view it as a treatment goal rather than thinking you have poor motivation to quit or a bad attitude. Anger is a predictable part of detoxification, and learning to cope with it can positively influence long-term abstinence.

TWENTY-THREE

The Costs and Benefits of Abstinence

Giving up the drug of choice is difficult at the best of times. Alcohol and drugs have been "friends" to many substance abusers. They helped numb pain, created a sense of belonging (for those who socialized in bars or used with friends), brought the illusion of happiness (however brief), gave instant courage, created the feeling of being powerful or in control, and may have been a source of substantial income for some.

EXERCISE: Costs and Benefits

This exercise is good if you are wondering what you would gain or lose by giving up your drug of choice. Simply brainstorm—list all the costs and benefits of using and not using. What do you learn from your list?

	Using	Abstinence
Costs		
Benefits		

RECOVERY AND THE GRIEVING PROCESS

Anger is an important and healthy part of accepting the loss of anything. During the anger stage, people can put some distance between themselves and the substance.

Consider the five stages of grief discussed earlier: denial, anger, bargaining, depression, and acceptance. Even a person who wants to stop using experiences great loss. During the anger stage of the grieving process, the big question is, "Why me?" If you are a recovering substance abuser, you're probably wondering how you will manage without the drug. In many ways, it is even more difficult to accept the loss of a drug than the loss of a life, because the substance is still available. The losses experienced by a recovering substance abuser may also include the loss of job, friends, family, hope, and perceived fun. In the beginning, at least, abstinence (not using at all) is not comfortable. You might get nervous and irritable. Anger is either internalized—resulting in guilt, low self-esteem, and depression, or externalized—resulting in aggression, blaming, mistrust, and resentment.

Anger is an important and healthy part of accepting the loss of anything. During the anger stage, people can put some distance between themselves and the addictive substance. Eventually, as new and healthier feelings and behaviors replace what the substance did, they are able to move toward acceptance. They do not forget the drug or alcohol, and the relationship or the hurt that contributed to their addiction, but they no longer have to feel angry, depressed, or preoccupied with the loss.

People who continue to "mourn" without acknowledging their anger (discussing and accepting the loss) may become "dry drunks." Although they are not drinking or using, they still have the same negative behavior and feelings. In other words, they are stuck in the anger stage of the mourning process, but without the substance that masked their torment.

TIPS FOR THE RECOVERING PERSON

- One of the first things you can do in recovering from a substance abuse is to normalize anger, and express it directly, with control.

- Expect to be anxious, more defensive and reactive, and realize that your tolerance level will be very low at times. Practice just "being" with uncomfortable feelings. Or take a walk, phone a friend, go to the park, write a letter.

- Assertiveness training and stress reduction techniques are a most important part of treatment regardless of the drug of choice. They reduce anger and over-reactions by increasing communication skill levels.

- Develop a spiritual component in your life—"turn it over." People have reported to me that believing in something other than the drug of choice has really helped in bad times. This has nothing to do with formal religions.

- Allow yourself to acknowledge your angry feelings in an individual or group counseling setting.

- Many treatment techniques include bashing a pillow or screaming as a way to encourage you to "let it all out." In my opinion, this is an ineffective technique, as it only teaches explosive forms of anger expression, and does nothing to address the initial cause, nor does it teach assertive communication. Get to the root of your anger.

- Learn how to cope with negative experiences.

- Realize that family members also have stored anger. There is often a false belief that if the substance abuse stops, all problems will be solved.

- Talk about how you are being affected by anger. Increase your own awareness.

Allow yourself to acknowledge your angry feelings in an individual or group counseling setting.

91

8

Anger and Healthy Boundary Development

TWENTY-FOUR

Abuse Issues: The Victimization Process

Children, and adults, need the safety and comfort of boundaries. If we grow up never knowing what to expect, if boundaries are constantly illogical, we may see ourselves as victims, or become abusers in turn. Children generally imitate what they experience. It's almost impossible for them to do something different, unless they use their anger to rebel. An abusive parent might think the angry child is "bad," but actually, to my mind, rebellion is a healthy response to an unhealthy situation.

Even one incident of violation such as rape, incest, or burglary can alter a person's boundary functioning in minutes. His or her world changes from a relatively safe place to a dangerous and unpredictable one (Nielson).

Many people cannot define what a boundary is, or what is considered abuse. A client once told me that a man lifted up her shirt "to have a peek." "Oh, that's nothing," she said. "He didn't mean anything by it. Don't get him in trouble." She obviously had experienced far more serious boundary violations if this incident was "nothing." She protected the fellow because she did not want disapproval and, in fact, told me that she was flattered by the attention.

When people have been victims of abuse, or are now abusers themselves, violation has become the norm. They have made "rules" (whether they recognize that or not) about how people should be treated, what behavior is acceptable, whether or not the right to privacy is to be respected, and who is in charge of one's boundaries. Many clients of social service agencies have become "stuck" in these rules and beliefs, even when they are not currently in abusive situations.

An abusive parent might think the angry child is "bad," but actually, to my mind, rebellion is a healthy response to an unhealthy situation.

95

DEFICIENT BOUNDARY DEVELOPMENT

Remember, anger is a signal that we need to pay attention to something that is emotionally or physically threatening. In other words, you could say that anger is our natural "boundary setter." The signal we get lets us know when a personal boundary has been crossed.

Boundary patterns are altered by several things. A child who grows up with caregivers who are chemically dependent or abusive encounters boundaries that are often inconsistent and illogical. One time it is all right to do something; another day the opposite is true. The child gets confused, and cannot distinguish appropriate boundaries. There are no rules, no consistency; the people who are supposed to be loving and trustworthy are unreliable.

EXAMPLES OF BOUNDARY VIOLATIONS

- When we need to defend ourselves in a threatening situation, such as verbal put-downs.

- When we experience physical, sexual, emotional, or any other kind of abuse.

- When a situation threatens our life or that of someone we love.

- When someone is manipulating or intimidating us.

- When we are touched in a way that makes us uncomfortable.

- When we are scolded for questioning authority.

- When we are taught to avoid conflict, and to please others.

- When we are told we are responsible for other people's feelings or behaviors.

- When others behave in an aggressive manner to get their way.

- When we are always agreeable, or appear to have no boundaries or self-respect.

- When we allow ourselves to be the victims of our children's abuse, or excuse or deny their inappropriate behavior.

SELF-HELP QUESTIONS: What Are Your Boundaries?

The following questions will help you discover why you may be having difficulties now in setting boundaries for yourself, with your children, or with other people.

What did you learn about boundaries in childhood?

1. When you were growing up, were you taught, and encouraged, to set boundaries relating to your privacy and your belongings?

2. Were you taught to regard your body as private?

3. Were your feelings, opinions, and needs respected? How do you know?

4. Were you taught to respect other people (or not to respect them) in the same way?

5. How do you think your childhood learnings have affected the way you treat your children now?

How do others treat you now? How do you treat others?

1. How would people describe you?

2. Have you ever been abused in any way by others? By whom?

3. Have you ever been abusive toward others? In what way?

4. How do you want to be treated by others?

5. Do you need to change the way you treat others? If so, how can you start?

6. How would you know if you were being treated badly? How would you respond?

What about trust?

1. Do you trust yourself? Explain why or why not.

2. Do you trust others? Explain why or why not.

TWENTY-FIVE

What Are Healthy Boundaries?

Boundaries are simply "guidelines," spoken and unspoken. They let others know our limits; help regulate closeness in relationships; tell people what we are, and are not, willing to do; and let us know when we are being threatened.

Boundaries let people know our needs and limits, while respecting the needs and limits of others.

Boundaries are not meant to punish or control others. They help us to avoid blaming someone by establishing the guidelines ahead of time. Boundaries let people know our needs and limits, while respecting the needs and limits of others. Boundaries are the basis for assertive communication.

SETTING HEALTHY BOUNDARIES

If you have not learned how to set boundaries with others, this will be challenging at first. Like riding a bicycle for the first time, it takes practice and determination not to give up. Others may not respond favorably. They may not know what these changes mean. They may think that you are abandoning them, or acting aloof.

Setting boundaries is done in a gentle, but firm, manner. Be direct. Most important, follow through!

Guidelines for Setting Healthy Boundaries

- Don't allow others to deny your reality. Trust what you think, feel, and hear.
- Don't allow others to speak for you. Let them know you can talk for yourself.
- Don't allow others to touch you, or touch others without asking permission.
- Don't abuse yourself or others in any way.

- Don't let the inappropriate boundary displays of others go unnoticed.

- Don't deny or ignore it when someone invades your boundaries.

- Don't allow others to tell you who you are, or direct your life.

- Don't fall in love or have sex with someone you have just met.

- Don't give too much of yourself away; you will not be appreciated.

- Don't manipulate people to get whatever you can out of them (using others).

- Don't allow others to take as much as they can from you (being used).

- Don't tell a stranger your whole life story when trust has not been established.

EVALUATING CHANGE IN AN ABUSIVE RELATIONSHIP

If you have been in an abusive situation, and are trying to improve it by setting healthy boundaries, the following questions will help you to determine whether or not your partner has changed his or her behavior. If you can answer yes to most of these questions, then you can have some assurance that you can begin to feel less threatened—your level of safety and security has increased.

Ask yourself the following questions about your partner:

- Does my partner express positive feelings to me, such as love and happiness, or are all his or her expressions related to anger?

- Am I allowed to make my own decisions and to be different from my partner?

- Am I able to pursue my interests without getting my partner's permission to do so?

- Does my partner listen and give me the respect I deserve when I say something that he or she does not agree with?

- Am I no longer afraid when I am around him or her?

- Do I feel safer because my partner no longer becomes violent or threatens violence against me or others?

- Does my partner get angry without being abusive—verbally or physically?

- When I get angry at my partner, does he or she refrain from attacking me?

- When we are discussing or negotiating something, does he or she do it without trying to control me or accuse me?

- Does my partner respect me and my right to say no?

- Does my partner no longer try to make up to me after a fight—with flowers or special gifts, for example?

- Do I no longer feel that my partner is trying to make me responsible for his or her frustration and anger?

9

Anger and Parenting: Keeping Your Cool

TWENTY-SIX

Triggers for Anger

Basically, there are three reasons why parents get angry: the child is not responding the way we want; our own personal needs are not being fulfilled due to our parental responsibilities; we don't know how to discipline without getting hooked into the child's bad mood.

Let's look at these three items individually. When a child does not do what we want, IT IS NORMAL. Save some grief by knowing that from the start. Then, use assertive skills to repeat your request and outline the consequences of not complying. The most important thing is to follow through with the consequences, so don't make them unrealistic as an over-reaction to how you feel. The goal here is to make it the child's problem, not yours. Your day does not have to be ruined by the child's misbehavior.

Next are our needs as parents and human beings. Most parents need friendships and socialization with other adults. We have a strong need for fun. It's not just kids who have fun! We need to get out and "do our own thing," too. We also crave solitude and perhaps the opportunity to read or pursue a hobby without being interrupted. We need freedom, not to be tied to a schedule day in and day out. And, finally, we need to feel good about ourselves; we need to be able to accomplish something as simple as watering our plants without having to stop and do something else.

The job of parenting makes great demands on us. Our needs are often put in the background, unless we deliberately plan for breaks as part of our schedule. Children have to learn that we need some time to ourselves, too. When my kids were small, they would "bombard" me at the door when I came home from work. I looked forward to this celebration of re-uniting, but after five minutes I would tell them I needed

Most parents need friendships and socialization with other adults.

The job of parenting makes great demands on us. Our needs are often put in the background...

The last main trigger for anger is a lack of knowledge about discipline.

ten minutes to rest before I started dinner. At first they didn't like it much, but it took only a few days for them to adjust to that boundary I set.

This type of "space" can give you time to switch gears and let go of work (taking off your work clothes can help). You can rest on the bed and meditate, or do nothing. Then, when you re-open the door, you, not the children, are in control.

Use the time with your kids to get out of the work mode. Celebrate their day and ask them to help you prepare dinner. If you have a baby and other young children tugging at you, set boundaries about what they can do, instead of giving in to the stress and getting angry.

The last main trigger for anger is a lack of knowledge about discipline. This can be remedied by learning assertive skills and parenting skills and practicing daily until your way of responding becomes comfortable and automatic. The kids will respond favorably, too. Sure, there will still be bad days, but at least you'll know how to respond, and your day won't be ruined.

MY TRIGGERS FOR ANGER

List three things your child does that makes you angry.	What will you do to handle each situation?
1.	
2.	
3.	

Let's face it—children can bring out the worst and the best in parents. They can test us to the limit, and melt our hearts the next minute. How is it that these little beings can wield so much power? I think the answer lies in two major areas. First, children are focused on finding ways to meet their needs, to get control over their environment by testing the limits in everything they do. Second, we parents have the same needs, and yet our role is to help (and even encourage) our children to "spread their wings" and find their power, without disrespecting the needs of others.

Let's face it— children can bring out the worst and the best in parents.

This is definitely a test for parents, because children challenge us while they are doing all this learning. We come to realize, perhaps, how vulnerable we are. They make us think about so many things that we haven't thought about before, such as what we truly value, why we are saying no, and why we get angry.

I've heard many parents say that they changed after they had kids. When asked in what way, the answer would often be, "I've turned into my mother!" or "I yell now, and I'm easily frustrated."

In my experience, we often need a trigger to bring out the "beast" (or the best) in us. Parenthood can do that. As a child, did you ever swear that you would never treat your child "like that"? Do you now find yourself doing what one of your parents did to you?

It is true that if we don't establish new values, we'll go by what we know. In other words, if you experienced "the silent treatment" when you misbehaved, you may use that style of parenting. Conversely, if you grew up in a family of "yellers," chances are you'll start screaming at your children.

Now, I must stress a point here. Not everybody follows this path. Sometimes, as children, we promise ourselves that we won't yell and, true enough, we don't. But what can happen is that we become reluctant to discipline and follow through with consequences, perhaps because we don't want to make our own children feel as bad as we once did. This parenting style doesn't work, either.

There is no set of parenting "rules" that is right for everyone. For example, some parents expect their children to wear socks or slippers in the house, while others insist on shoes. Those types of guidelines won't harm the child. What is harmful is inconsistency in routines and rules, emotional or physical abuse, or inconsistent

Guiding means to lead the way, so we need to be clear in our own minds about what we value as ground rules.

parental behavior, when one parent says one thing and the other something else. This only teaches children how to manipulate, and probably results in arguments between the parents.

Many parents feel that discipline must include spanking, "to teach a lesson." My personal opinion is that hitting a child only teaches that you can influence others by using physical force. It becomes "normal" for the child, who probably will treat his or her own children the same way, or under-react for fear of hurting them. If we all could take a parenting course on how to discipline, I wonder if the increasing violence reported in schools would drop.

In summary, we need to find a consistent way to discipline, not punish, so that we never have to feel guilty about guiding our children's behavior. Guiding means to lead the way, so we need to be clear in our own minds about what we value as ground rules.

TWENTY-SEVEN

Helping Children Deal with Anger

When children get angry, they often don't know what else to do, because they can't express what they want or feel. It's often a guessing game for us to determine what their anger really means. For example, a child colors on the wall. She or he knows there is plenty of paper. You ask yourself, "Why would the kid do that? What's the intent behind that behavior?"

There may be a great deal of meaning behind it. It could be that the child wants attention. It could mean that the child is bored, tired, or hungry. Now if we just get angry and clean it up, nothing is taught or learned. We need to give the child, no matter how young, a vocabulary for feelings. We do this by saying, for example, "Sue, you look bored, but coloring on the wall is not allowed. If you want to do something that's fun, just ask Mom (or Dad)." Then you and Sue clean the wall.

I know this works. I've done it when my kids were very young. If one of them was having a temper tantrum, I'd say, "You look like you need a hug. When you're ready, Mom will hug you." Then I'd get busy and soon, by gum, my child was asking for a hug (or gesturing if he or she didn't talk well). I'd use the hug to reinforce the positive way of getting what we need, instead of getting mad. Eventually, they would just ask for what they needed, instead of acting out.

Here are some other things that work well with children. They love "exercises" because you are interacting with them. You can learn a lot about an angry child who cannot, or will not, discuss feelings with you if you try activities such as the following.

When children get angry, they often don't know what else to do, because they can't express what they want or feel.

109

Coloring

Have your child draw a picture of his or her anger. Ask questions, such as, "Why did you choose those colors? What do they mean?" or "Why did you draw ...?" or "Do you know why you got angry?" Put the picture up on the bulletin board or refrigerator.

Play Therapy

A young child would love to play house or dolls with you. This enables you to use dolls and other props to help the child express feelings.

Choose a typical situation when your child gets angry. Ask the child to pick a doll to represent him- or herself. Ask the child who you should be, and what other people should be included in your "play."

Ask the child what the people in the house do when (describe the situation that upsets the child). Then act out the scene, letting the child lead the way. Use the opportunity to help the child find words that identify the reasons for the anger, such as tired, lonely, or bored.

Then teach new ways to handle anger by suggesting that the child tell you what he or she needs when these feelings happen. Give some words to the anger, as in the examples above. Set guidelines to prevent abusive behavior.

Sculpting

Using clay or play dough, ask the child to "mold" feelings such as fear, sadness, or disappointment. Perhaps you might like to do the same, and compare your "sculptures."

RECIPE FOR PLAY DOUGH

1 cup water	1 cup flour
1/2 cup salt	2 tablespoons oil
1 teaspoon cream of tartar	food coloring

Heat all ingredients on very low heat, stirring constantly. Cook until they form a ball. Remove from heat, cool slightly, and knead the dough until it is smooth.

Cool very well before storing in air-tight containers or zip-lock bags.

This recipe makes soft play dough which will keep a long time if it is not allowed to dry out. You don't need to refrigerate it.

Acting

Suggest that your child think of some feelings and then "freeze" in positions that illustrate these feelings, to see if you can guess what they are. Or, as an alternative, have the child model opposite feelings, such as happiness and sadness. Ask the child which alternative she or he is feeling, and why.

You could also ask the child to act out his or her emotions, using either facial expressions or gestures that involve the whole body.

This exercise and those described above not only teach, but also help you and your child bond and have fun, and give your child individual attention, which might just decrease everyone's anger!

Increasing Your Child's "Feelings" Vocabulary

Children can learn that they have many feelings. Often, they act out in angry or destructive ways when they cannot ask for what they need because they don't know the words to describe what they are feeling.

Help children to recognize when they are bored, scared, tired, or need attention. Offer suggestions, or get them involved in constructive activities.

Always let them know that abusive behavior is not appropriate or tolerated! Be firm, but caring—let them know that they can choose to have control.

Always let them know that abusive behavior is not appropriate or tolerated! Be firm, but caring—let them know that they can choose to have control.

TWENTY-EIGHT

Effective Discipline Skills

The goal is to teach the child acceptable boundaries of behavior— a lifelong resource.

The key word here is discipline. It means to educate, not punish. The goal is to teach the child acceptable boundaries of behavior—a lifelong resource. You are teaching the child how to treat you and others, and to respect property.

The lesson includes teaching that all behavior that we choose has natural consequences. As parents, we must convey that it is the behavior that your children choose that causes you to follow through with the consequences. You are not "out to get them," or make their little lives horrible for no reason. (I know they sometimes think that!)

These guidelines may help you to teach your child.

1. Model assertive skills.

Children often get angry when they don't know how to deal with threats, name-calling, or other inappropriate behavior. Practice and model appropriate responses, such as, "I don't like it when you call me names. Please stop."

Try not to get hooked into solving "who-done-it" scenes. If your child wants you to be judge and jury, tell the child how to stand up for him- or herself.

For example, Sarah runs to you after Jimmy takes her crayon. She wants you to punish Jimmy for "stealing a crayon." Ask Sarah to tell Jimmy, "I don't like it when you take my crayon. Please give it back, or I won't play with you." Tell Sarah that if Jimmy does not give back the crayon, she must follow through. Jimmy learns the lesson that not playing fairly results in playing alone.

You are showing your child how to use assertive skills to teach other people how she or he wants to be treated. Assertive skills are an invaluable tool that can be used anytime, anywhere, throughout the child's life.

2. *Set boundaries.*

Children need to know that you have a right to private time. Parents can get angry and "burned out" when they allow their children to monopolize all of their time.

Tell your child you need ten minutes by yourself, then relax without guilt!

Never allow aggressive or verbally abusive behavior. Teach the child acceptable ways to express displeasure.

3. *Establish predetermined consequences.*

Parents often get angry at children for not listening, and may threaten over and over to punish them. The children, who will naturally test the limits, repeat the undesirable behaviors until the parents lose their temper. Sound familiar?

Children need and respond well to clear, predetermined consequences, such as, "I will take the ball away if you bounce it again in the house." Then FOLLOW THROUGH!

When we get angry at our children, we are actually angry at ourselves for feeling out of control, or powerless.

4. *Give the child more responsibility.*

When they act out, children may be signaling us that they are maturing and need more challenges. By giving them chores or tasks that they are capable of doing well, you can meet their need to feel that they are an important part of the family.

For example, give the child the job of feeding a pet, or wiping the table, or helping out in some other way. You may want to post a list of daily responsibilities so the child can check them off after completing them.

At the end of the week, you can give the child an age-appropriate reward, such as a privilege, a small toy, a special activity with a parent, or a movie.

5. *Help the child out of a bad mood.*

Use humor or a hug, or distract the child with an activity he or she enjoys. Tell the child you love him or her. Children need to hear those reassuring words often, and may be unhappy because they want attention or affection.

6. Use the "time-out" method.

Children love us for giving them the structure and safety net that discipline provides.

When children misbehave, tell them that they need a time-out to think about what they've done. Ask them to sit in a chair (never in a corner!) for about two minutes if they are young. Remember how short their attention span is, and the fact that this isn't intended to be punishment, but a reflective pause.

When they sit down, say, "You are on the chair because you (describe the child's behavior), and you can get up in two minutes. I will start your time when you let me know you're ready." Use your microwave or kitchen timer so they can hear it go off.

Then, ask them to explain why they were on the chair. If they can't, tell them why, and then say you will time them again. Believe me, it won't take long for them to remember!

Now, this scenario went off perfectly, but sometimes our children don't believe that we would do such a horrible thing, and get up from the chair, or talk throughout their time-out. Remind them that you will start the time when they are ready, but they cannot do anything else until after the time-out. In other words, all privileges are put on hold.

I can remember when our four-year-old was being timed-out, and later that day our toddler did something wrong. I just said no, but he wanted to be timed-out, too! So I obliged him, and he sat for 30 seconds and was happy.

Children love us for giving them the structure and safety net that discipline provides. I think the most important thing to remember about discipline is that you are teaching your kids to think for themselves about the consequences of their actions. That is empowerment. If we always tell them what to do, they never learn for themselves, and chances are, they will keep listening to others instead of being able to make up their own minds.

TWENTY-NINE

Routines and Rituals

Routines are activities that are performed in the same way at the same time every day. They provide structure, and are very comforting to children. With routines, they know what to expect, as sure as the sun will always rise and set. Routines also help them get into regular work, play, and sleep patterns, which helps us, too!

Routines...provide structure, and are very comforting to children.

For instance, it is important to end the day with a moment of bonding. Some children cannot go to sleep without a bedtime story, which actually can trigger the brain to fall asleep when the story is done. I know it works for me! I read the story, and I start getting really tired.

Rituals are special customs or ways to celebrate or remember important occasions. They can be associated with holidays, such as Thanksgiving, or you can develop them especially for family events, such as birthdays.

Consider adopting some of the following routines and rituals in your home:

- Have dinner at the same time every day, if at all possible.

- Allow your children 20 to 30 minutes of reading time before you turn out the lights. You may have to send them to bed that much earlier, but most kids appreciate the fact that the lights don't go off immediately.

- Enjoy events like "family night," when you order pizza and watch a movie, or play a board game.

- Have special brunches on the weekend, when there is more time to cook.

- Once a week, let your child(ren) decide what you will have for dinner.

- Light a candle at dinner time, or have a child make up a prayer.

- There are numerous seasonal rituals that children need and love. If you can't decide how to celebrate holidays, ask your child to suggest ideas, or borrow a book from the library.

THIRTY

Understanding Your Teen

Teens are probably going through the hardest time of their lives.

From my own experience, research, and speaking with parents, it seems that the adolescent period is like a roller-coaster ride of mixed emotions. The level of stress and tension in the home often escalates, leading to frustration and anger for both teens and their parents. It is normal to question yourself when you see behavior that is not easy to understand. It can be very confusing and challenging. I try to remind myself that I am not alone in the challenge—my children are also experiencing emotions they can't understand.

The struggle for autonomy and independence can be very powerful for your teen. This important transition from childhood to adulthood can start as early as age 10, depending on the child's physical maturity and childhood experiences.

Teens are probably going through the hardest time of their lives. They are dealing with hormonal changes, pimples, and the urge to be independent, yet they need us so much (but don't expect them to tell you that). They are trying to figure out their "style." Do they follow everyone else, or lead the pack? Do they listen to you or to their friends? They want freedom, and guidance.

It's hard for parents to let go and trust more. We realize just how little power we actually have. A hard-handed approach will certainly be met with resistance. A soft approach can backfire, too. Your teen needs to know that you are still in control, but are reasonable about giving more responsibility. Here are a few survival tips:

- Reframe your belief that your teen is rebellious on purpose. It is natural for teens to want to find their own style—and it won't be the same as yours!

- Respect your differences as long as your teen is suggesting things that would not harm him- or herself, other people, or personal property.

- When your teen asks for your honest opinion, give your honest opinion. Also point out that it's okay for the two of you to disagree; love is not the issue here.

- When teens break rules, parents must decide on logical consequences. For example, if they come in one hour late, the next time they must come home one hour early. Tell them that they made this happen through their own actions. Do not "own" their problems or get angry. Point out that their behavior caused you to worry about their safety. Also emphasize that they broke a verbal agreement by being late. Trust must be earned.

Suggestions for consequences for irresponsible or destructive behavior:

– No TV for ….	– Extra chores
– No stereo for….	– Volunteer work
– No phone for….	– Paying for destruction out of allowance
– No car for….	– No allowance
	– Ask them to suggest their own consequences!

- Teens want to be respected as "adult," yet they still need your love and guidance. Discipline, don't punish. Punishment means you are owning their problems, and they know it. They can push back even harder, and nobody wins. Tell them that they are choosing (through the behavior) the extent of the freedom and trust they want.

- Don't sweat the little stuff. For example, my 13-year-old wanted to wear make-up. I said yes, with some restrictions. She wore it for two weeks and lost interest because "it was too much work." If I had said no, without discussing it, she would probably have wanted it even more, or "snuck it" (like I did as a teen).

- Listen to teens. They may be giving you feedback about how your actions or attitude are affecting them. Don't be defensive; acknowledge their honesty. You don't have to agree, but praise them for speaking non-defensively to you.

- Reward good behavior through praise and increased responsibility or freedom.

- Tell teens you love them. Because they may now shun kisses and hugs (they aren't cool), tell them you won't show affection in public, but you will in private. Don't think that because teens tell you they're "too old for that," that they don't want to be touched or shown that they are special.

- Tell teens that you value honesty from them. I remember when I was going to a Christmas party, and my father told me to call him if I got drunk. He said I would not get in trouble for phoning for a ride and being honest, but I would lose car privileges if I drove after drinking. Well, I was scared to phone because I thought he would go back on his word, but I called him anyway. He said nothing, except to thank me for phoning, and tell me he loved me. That moment will always remain a fond memory of love and trust.

- Learn when to back off if things get heated. Anger energy can be powerful. Unhook; someone has to stop. Show your child how.

117

THIRTY-ONE

De-Escalating Anger in Teens

Anger can be just as frightening a feeling for the people who express it as it is for those around them.

As the parent of two teens, plus one pre-teen who is an "early bloomer," I can sympathize with the parents who call seeking advice on how to deal with an angry, belligerent, or acting-out teen. The most common questions are, "Why is my kid acting like this?" and "What have I/we done wrong?"

Some cooperative children become expressive, oppositional teens, while some outspoken, hard-to-handle children become silent teens. Both situations are normal. Like the under-reacting (passive) and over-reacting (aggressive) behaviors discussed earlier in this book, both are fear-based communication stances. Your teen's greatest fear is of looking and sounding "un-cool" or foolish. In this section we will look at the angry, aggressive teen, and in the next section we'll consider the silent teen.

Anger can be just as frightening a feeling for the people who express it as it is for those around them. As a parent, teacher, or caregiver, you can help angry teens deal with their anger constructively and safely.

First of all, determine whether the anger being expressed is legitimate anger (which is about injustice, boundary violations, or other unfair acts) or exaggerated anger (which is usually about frustration, pain, or fear) (Fletcher, p. 35). The difference is important in terms of how the anger is expressed.

Legitimate anger is more likely to be expressed verbally, while exaggerated anger is much more volatile. The teen may yell, swear, flail his or her arms around, make grand body gestures, blame, act aggressively, or be completely out of control.

When working with angry teens, it is important to ensure their safety and that of others. Asking other teens or children in the house to leave serves two purposes. First, the anger energy, which we discussed earlier, is lessened when there isn't an audience. Often friends or siblings will take sides or join in the "battle" to show allegiance. If you don't separate the teens, you may well be dealing with two or more angry people. The other purpose for dismissing others is to allow the angry person some personal space.

Many years ago I worked with young offenders who were "corralled" into one day room. This was a recipe for disaster. These kids were hopping mad at being arrested and losing their freedom and privileges. They often fed on the anger of others, and the emotional environment was usually tense, and potentially volatile. As staff members, we were taught to always keep our backs to the wall and make sure there was a pathway to the exit. Very sound advice. On numerous occasions, those rules probably saved my life or, at the very least, kept me out of hospital. To this day, I still find myself taking the "wall" seat at a restaurant, and as an addictions counselor, I always place my chair nearest the exit. Old habits die hard!

When a teen is really angry, you can de-escalate the situation by remaining calm yourself, listening to what he or she is saying, and, most important, being aware of your own body posture. Let's look at two examples of how you can handle an enraged teen.

When working with angry teens, it is important to ensure their safety and that of others.

First, let's assume you are a teacher in a classroom setting and an angry student is pounding the desk and yelling. Don't stand over the student, which is a threatening, authoritarian stance, but kneel down and make eye contact to show the student you are listening. I would come right out and state my feelings about the behavior, for example, "Tom, right now your anger is scaring me. You have a right to have angry feelings, but I'm concerned that your angry behavior will result in your hurting yourself or someone else." Then, I would find out what the real problem is by asking questions. This is an assertive technique of "inquiring," which will be discussed in more detail later. Basically, you start by asking broad questions and then narrow down the issues until the real problem is defined.

We might think they have nothing to get that upset about, but remember your own adolescence, when a bad hair day or pimples meant that your life was coming to an end.

For the second example, we'll assume the teen is at home, swearing, name-calling, and making verbal or physical threats toward you, the parent. Separate the angry teen by asking any siblings to leave the room. You may want to have your spouse or another adult nearby to be supportive or to call on if things get out of hand.

Again, I would begin by stating my feelings about the behavior. If I find it frightening, I would say so. If the teen is name-calling or being destructive, I would set some boundaries by saying, for example, "I want to understand your concerns and try to help, but verbally attacking me or destroying things in the house is not okay and does nothing to solve the problem."

It is often calming and less threatening to teens if you sit down and invite them to do the same (although they'll often refuse), so you can "help them sort out the problem." I've had better results not by being authoritarian, but by facilitating a process.

I tend to use a little humor, which is intended to reframe the situation and take the edge off. Too much humor might be taken to indicate that you are making light of the situation. Teens often view their life events as very serious or "heavy." We might think they have nothing to get that upset about, but remember your own adolescence, when a bad hair day or pimples meant that your life was coming to an end.

During your discussion, try to put words to the teens' feelings. As with young children, this gives them more information, and a vocabulary they can use to describe their anger. Explore conflict resolution options. This helps them to gain control by choosing a plan of action instead of reacting.

As you are building trust and rapport through this respectful process, you may ask a teen if you can touch his or her shoulder. I can't say enough about the power of a simple touch. It is very healing and calming, to people of all ages.

Often teens, like younger children who act out, are bored, or telling us that they need more responsibility or trust. Try giving them a task, asking them to assist you, or letting them have more responsibility, with clear expectations defined. This enables them to establish their trustworthiness.

Always address disruptive behaviors of any kind; do not ignore them. If ignored, teens may escalate their behavior in an attempt to get our attention. Help teens identify underlying feelings associated with the acting-out or bored behavior. You can do this by saying, for example, "Jane, I've noticed your behavior [describe what you see]. What are you feeling right now? When did you become [describe the feeling]?" This technique helps teens to sort out their feelings, while not projecting them onto others, as so often happens. It also serves to help the teen stay "grounded."

Give angry teens choices and allow them to explore their own options.

Give angry teens choices and allow them to explore their own options. This helps to pull them out of their negative behavior. Ask them what the consequences of their behavior ought to be. I have found that my children give themselves harder consequences than I would have chosen!

Trust yourself— don't let their fears become your fears.

All these techniques are intended to teach teens the art of negotiation, of taking responsibility for their behavior instead of projecting anger and blaming others. They also help teens establish boundaries and give them skills to cope with the bad times. Your matter-of-fact, understanding, and confident approach serves to increase trust and enhance bonding with your child. If you use this approach consistently, your teen will have better self-esteem and more respect for you.

THIRTY-TWO

What about the Silent Teen?

Sometimes teens don't open up because they don't feel safe.

Silence is a form of communication. It can tell us that a teen is afraid of sounding foolish, afraid of being out of control, or playing the "I won't talk to you" game, which is a powerful way to gain control of a situation.

Many silent teens keep their thoughts to themselves and try to work out their own problems. They may look sullen, withdrawn, and sad. Parents may respond with anxious efforts to "do something" or they may eventually give up trying, because teens often can hold out longer than we can!

The following tips may help you to cope with and assist a silent teen:

- Avoid projecting your own feelings of helplessness onto the situation.

- Do not take everything personally. In most cases, this is not about you.

- Remember that the teen is afraid of looking like a fool. He or she might be trying to make you look foolish instead of facing his or her own fears.

- Try to engage the teen in playing a board game, baking a cake, discussing music.

- You might want to remain silent yourself. Don't try to pry communication out of your teen. Act casual, get busy, comment on the weather or something unrelated to the problem.

- Try a little humor. Laugh at yourself, or a situation in your lives—but never at your teen!

- Develop trust by developing rapport. Sometimes teens don't open up because they don't feel safe.

Remember that life is very serious for teens. They often assume the worst and are really afraid of being let down. The best advice is to be consistent, to be loving, to set reasonable boundaries, to develop trust, and to help teens acquire open, direct communication skills. Be a good role model. If your own self-esteem is low, you will act unsure and your teen will react accordingly. Trust yourself—don't let their fears become your fears.

10

Communicating Assertively

THIRTY-THREE

Three Components of Assertiveness

Assertiveness has three basic components:

1. Knowledge (to know how)
2 Skill (to be able)
3. Attitude (to be willing)

If any one of these components is missing, following through with being assertive is highly unlikely. For example, if someone teaches you how something is done, you have the knowledge, but if you don't have the skills or the will to do it, or if you don't believe that you can do it, the likelihood of attaining your goal is slim.

As a counselor, I meet many people who feel that things will change positively for them just because they've entered treatment. If they say, "I'll practice after I leave," I can predict that nothing much will be different. Maybe you know people who repeatedly enter counseling, although nothing seems to change for them. There is the illusion of work, but if they do not develop the skills or the attitude needed to make the changes, nothing changes! This is true not only of attaining assertion skills; it also applies to anger management, parenting, or any other goal desired.

Let's start by gaining some knowledge about assertiveness by defining it. What does assertiveness look like in comparison to other communication styles?

> *...if someone teaches you how something is done, you have the knowledge, but if you don't have the skills or the will to do it, or if you don't believe that you can do it, the likelihood of attaining your goal is slim.*

Definition of Assertiveness
Assertiveness is an attitude that allows you to act in your best interest, express honest feelings, and exercise your personal rights, without denying the rights of others.

The voices of assertive people are firm, but warm and relaxed.

What does assertiveness sound like? (verbal signs)

1. The voices of assertive people are firm, but warm and relaxed.

2. They are able to refuse a request and say no without feeling guilty.

3. They are able to stick with the conversation.

4. They can request behavior changes from others.

What does assertiveness look like? (non-verbal signs)

1. Assertive people make eye contact—not staring, but looking away periodically.

2. Their posture is straight, more open, and relaxed.

3. Their facial expressions are relaxed.

4. They gesture with their hands while they talk.

THIRTY-FOUR

A Comparison of Communication Styles

PASSIVE (under-reacting)	ASSERTIVE (direct, open)	AGGRESSIVE (over-reacting)
Fear-based.	Self-assured.	Fear-based.
Person looks, sounds timid, shy, insecure.	Person looks, sounds confident, gentle.	Person looks, sounds angry, intimidating.
Silently angry at self and others for being taken advantage of.	Able to say no and set boundaries.	Sets boundaries by overt anger.
When hurt, keeps it in, blames self.	When hurt, resolves issues, discusses feelings.	When hurt, hurts others.
When angry, gets even in "silent" ways.	When angry, handles problems openly.	When angry, blames others.
Feels powerless, controlled by others.	Feels in control.	Feels powerless, controls others.
Dislikes self.	Likes self, others.	Dislikes others.
Drawn to compulsive behaviors to avoid problems.	Copes effectively with problems.	Drawn to compulsive behaviors to avoid problems.
Lonely, apologetic.	At ease with self, open, honest, direct.	Lonely inside, angry, blames others.
Cautious, unconfident, indirect.	Honest, open, responsible.	Violates rights of others.

SELF-HELP WORKSHEET: Anger Communication

Anger is a very basic human emotion that plays an important role in the way we communicate with others. The following questions offer you an opportunity to make an objective self-study of how anger affects you and how you deal with it in your daily life. This increased awareness on your part may help you feel more comfortable with yourself and improve your relationships with others.

1. Do you admit that you are angry when asked by someone else?

2. Do you tend to take your anger out on someone other than the person you are angry with?

3. When you are angry with someone, do you discuss it with that person?

4. Do you keep things in until you finally "explode" with anger?

5. Do you pout or sulk for a long time (several days) when someone hurts your feelings?

6. Can you disagree with others even though you think they might get angry?

7. Do you hit others when you get angry?

8. Does it upset you a great deal when someone disagrees with you?

9. Do you express your ideas when they differ from those of others?

10. Do you have a tendency to be very critical of others?

11. Are you satisfied with the way you settle your differences with others?

12. Is it very difficult for you to say nice things to other people?

13. Do you have good control of your temper?

14. Do you become depressed very easily?

15. Do you have frequent arguments with others?

16. Do you sometimes feel angry at someone you love?

17. Do you ever have a strong urge to do something harmful?

18. Do you keep your cool (control) when you are angry with someone?

19. Do you tend to feel very bad or very guilty after getting angry at someone?

20. When you become angry, do you pull away or withdraw from people?

21. When someone is angry with you, do you automatically or quickly strike back with your own feelings of anger?

22. Do you have difficulty saying no and then feel angry at the other person for imposing on you?

After assessing your answers, do you think you have a problem with anger?

_____

Is there a "theme" to your anger (in relationships, with people in authority, for example)? _____

THIRTY-FIVE

Conflict Is Normal in Relationships

Anger, like love, is a very powerful feeling. Anger comes out in relationships when there is a gap between what we want or need from someone close to us and what we are actually getting. Anger in a relationship isn't necessarily a bad thing, for it can provide the energy for honest communication. It is destructive, however, when it is used as a source of power or a defensive, blaming, or controlling behavior. Sometimes, the relationship suffers greatly due to hidden anger, which was discussed in Chapter 2. Signs of unexpressed anger may be an unfulfilling or even nonexistent sex life, lack of energy, and inability to get close.

A helpful way to reduce excessive anger in a relationship may be to figure out what the "feeling" part of the anger is about. Is there an unresolved fear of abandonment? Is your autonomy or self-esteem being threatened? Do you have a fear of failure? Is your physical safety being threatened? Ask yourself if your anger comes out when you communicate: do you order, command, threaten, criticize, blame, withdraw, or use excessive humor?

Recognizing and admitting your anger is the first step. Then, expressing your feelings directly and honestly whenever possible reduces stored anger. Let the other person know the feeling part of the anger. Say, for example, "I am hurt by what you said." Let the person know what you need.

Remember, anger can give us a wonderful source of energy to change a situation for the better, or it can destroy us. The secret lies in what you choose to do with that energy. Feeling angry toward loved ones doesn't mean that we don't love them.

The choice is not "Do you want conflict or don't you want it?" but, rather, "Where, when, and how much conflict do you want?" We don't have the option to avoid conflict, but we do have a choice as to how we will handle it. Failure to deal with anger may destroy the love that was once there, because if you repress feelings of anger, you inevitably squelch all feelings, especially feelings of love. Confronting the other person should not be seen as a sign of hostility. Rather, it indicates you care enough to want to work out problems. The love is usually strengthened.

It is important to realize that dealing with anger effectively decreases your fear of anger and increases self-esteem through the direct expression of feelings and needs. Dealing with anger helps you feel in control. You are in a better position to get needs met, while setting healthy boundaries in relationships.

130

THIRTY-SIX

Assertive Skill Development

Assertive behavior is a very effective way to deal with anger. It is self-expressive and not harmful to others. Assertiveness is a learned skill. You don't just become assertive as you get older, although certain personality styles appear to be more naturally assertive than others. For instance, some people are more outgoing and dominant by nature, while others are shy, go-along-with-the-crowd types. But remember, the fact that a person is outgoing does not guarantee that he or she will practice assertive behaviors!

Assertion, when used properly, is very gentle and non-threatening. Although assertion is often confused with aggression, you are probably not being assertive if you raise your voice and make demands.

There are many positive consequences of using assertive techniques, such as being able to handle manipulation, being able to say no, and being able to manage someone else's anger, as well as your own. Assertive behaviors improve communication and often lead you to more satisfying relationships or, conversely, allow you to respond appropriately to unhealthy ones (which may mean leaving a relationship). Ultimately, assertive behaviors increase self-esteem and confidence, while decreasing fear, anger, and guilt.

The following are five different techniques for being assertive. Each one is good in specific circumstances. You will find that you automatically combine some, which is normal. Your first attempts to be assertive should be made in a safe situation, when things aren't "heated up." Practice for fun, to get used to what you are doing. Keep trying, even if the other person does not change. Remember, the purpose of being assertive

Assertion, when used properly, is very gentle and non-threatening.

131

It took you many months to learn to walk, and it can also take a long time to learn new behaviors.

is not to get your way all the time; it is to enable you to set boundaries with others, and to feel comfortable about expressing your feelings and needs.

Another important reason why assertiveness is a good skill to practice is that by being assertive, you are telling your unconscious mind that you deserve to be treated fairly. You are important, and your right to express your needs directly is essential to self-esteem.

Don't give up too soon. Other people need time to get used to the "new you." They may even try some old ways to see if you really mean what you say. Stick with it. It took you many months to learn to walk, and it can also take a long time to learn new behaviors.

The five assertive skills are explained in the following pages. After reading about each one, describe a situation you are facing in order to personalize and practice these skills.

ASSERTIVE SKILL 1: BROKEN RECORD

When to Use: Refusing a request (saying no)

Sticking to a goal or desired outcome

Method: Speak in a calm, relaxed voice.

Calmly repeat over and over what you want.

Speak in a low, "matter-of-fact" voice.

Do not give up or lose your temper.

Example 1: (Refusing a request)

"I understand what you are saying, but I'm not interested."

"I'm still not interested."

Note: If someone is being extremely manipulative and refuses to take no for an answer, try saying, "I've said no, please respect my decision."

Example 2: (Sticking to your goal)

"I would like you to pick up your toys now."

"I know you don't want to, but the toys have to be picked up."

Give an example of when you could use this skill.

_____

_____

_____

_____

_____

ASSERTIVE SKILL 2: AVOIDING DEFENSIVENESS

When to Use: Accepting manipulative criticism comfortably

Agreeing with the truth or possibility of truth

Agreeing with logic

Method: Calmly acknowledge the truth without becoming anxious or getting hooked in.

Allow another person to state an opinion without defending yourself.

Speak in an "I don't care" tone, as if the comment were water off a duck's back.

Example 1:   (Agree with the truth.)

They say: "You are short."

You say: "I know I am short."

Example 2:   (Agree with the possibility of the truth, however slight.)

They say: "You are sloppy."

You say: "Perhaps I am sloppy."

Give an example of when you could use this skill.

_____

_____

_____

_____

_____

_____

ASSERTIVE SKILL 3: RESPONDING TO CRITICISM

When to Use: Accepting your errors, without having to apologize

Responding to criticism by admitting an error

Method: Respond calmly; do NOT apologize.

Separate the mistake (your behavior) from yourself as a person.

Example: They say: "You forgot to file these papers."

You say: "Yes, I did forget. I'm usually more responsible."

Note: Contrary to popular belief, it is not "polite" to apologize abjectly for every little error. You are human, and nobody is perfect. It is okay to make a mistake.

Nevertheless, this assertive technique will not be very effective if you have made the same mistake repeatedly in the past. For instance, if you always forget to "file the papers," you really can't say, "I'm usually more responsible."

Give an example of when you could use this skill.

_____

_____

_____

_____

_____

_____

_____

_____

ASSERTIVE SKILL 4: INQUIRING ABOUT THE REAL PROBLEM

When to Use: Clarifying what the underlying problem is

Asking for more information

Breaking the manipulation

Method: Ask specific questions about the concern.

Keep on topic without counter-attacking.

Listen, without defending yourself.

Keep probing to get at the underlying issue.

Example: They say: "You're always busy."

You say: "I don't understand why it bothers you that I'm busy."

They say: "You never do anything with us anymore."

You say: "What would you like to do that we're not doing?"

Note: Most conflicts never get resolved because one person hears an accusatory statement and counter-attacks. The argument really begins to "take off" when other issues are drawn into the discussion!

Give an example of when you could use this skill.

_____

_____

_____

_____

_____

ASSERTIVE SKILL 5: DESCRIBING YOUR FEELINGS

When to Use: Telling someone something important that is difficult to say

Letting someone know what behavior changes you need to see

Responding to a person who intimidates you

Method: Write out the dialogue (message) you would like to say. You can read it out loud to keep yourself on track. This helps you to be non-defensive and keep to the point.

Examples: Describe the behavior: "Whenever you are angry, you call me names."

Express your feelings: "I feel that you don't respect me."

Specify what behavior changes you want: "I would like you to tell me your concerns without putting me down."

State the consequences:

Positive outcome: "If you can tell me why you are upset without putting me down, our relationship will be better."

Negative outcome: "If you can't stop putting me down, I will feel that you don't care about our relationship and eventually I will leave."

Write your own "script" for a real problem.

_____

_____

_____

_____

_____

THIRTY-SEVEN

Attitude Changes

Your attitude is based on what you believe about yourself.

People can read all about assertion and take many courses, but they will not be able to change their behavior, or be able to integrate assertive techniques, until they shift old beliefs.

Your attitude is based on what you believe about yourself. For example, if you do not believe that you have the right to set boundaries with others, it will be extremely difficult for you to stick up for yourself when others treat you badly. You might believe that you will lose a friend or partner if you say no. Most people think they are angry with others, when actually they are more upset with themselves for not being able to stand up for their own rights!

Altering one's beliefs is the hardest internal change to make, for several reasons. Firstly, we are creatures of habit, and often resist change, even though we know intellectually the change may be for the better. It feels safer emotionally to hang on to old baggage, coping by using familiar defenses.

You have the right to see, hear, and feel without having your perceptions denied by others.

Secondly, you may have to let go of how you currently "define" or picture yourself, such as a scapegoat, victim, or warrior. People who believe they are victims, for example, may at times unknowingly and unconsciously put themselves in situations where they will most likely be victimized. The attitude of a victim says, "I don't deserve to exercise my personal rights."

Thirdly, changing your attitude and beliefs may mean that you will actually have to allow yourself to feel anger, bringing it to the surface in order to help yourself exercise your personal rights or ask for what you need.

The next page identifies some rights that everyone is entitled to. This is just a partial list. You may want to add more.

BASIC HUMAN RIGHTS

You have the right:

- to be treated with respect.
- to not have to justify your behavior.
- to say no without feeling guilty.
- to take time to think.
- to feel good about yourself.
- to form and express your own opinions.
- to be left alone, to choose not to assert yourself.
- to decide what to do with your time.
- to see, hear, and feel without having your perceptions denied by others.
- to express your feelings in ways that do not abuse other people.
- to change your mind.
- to make mistakes.
- to say "I don't care."
- to be listened to and taken seriously.
- to say "I don't understand."
- to ask for what you want.

EXERCISE: Assertive Attitude

What I currently believe about my rights

(List all your rights.)

_____

_____

_____

_____

_____

_____

_____

_____

_____

What I can add to my current belief system

(Add more rights to your list.)

_____

_____

_____

_____

_____

_____

_____

11

Steps in Dealing with Anger

THIRTY-EIGHT

Your Own Anger

Learning to handle your anger involves ongoing practice and perhaps some hard work and determination, until the technique you choose becomes a natural response. Anger management is more than just handling an explosive situation. It is an ongoing process of understanding yourself, your needs, how you choose to behave, your lifestyle, and your value judgments. It also involves reducing your stored anger. The following guidelines will help you to manage your own anger more constructively.

Anger management is more than just handling an explosive situation.

1. Recognize that you are angry.

Acknowledging our feelings puts us directly in touch with what bothers, hurts, or angers us. This first step may be the hardest. This is because anger is a defense mechanism which is designed to protect us from unpleasant or uncomfortable feelings or memories.

- **Own your anger.**

  Acknowledging anger and claiming anger as your own increases self-awareness and prevents blaming others. Turning blame into "I" statements locates the anger where it actually is, inside of you.

- **Develop early warning signs.**

  Pay attention to physical clues that indicate you are angry. You may tense up in the chest area and notice a change in your breathing. Or your stomach may become "nervous" and even start hurting. Notice if your heart is beating faster, or your palms are sweating. These are physiological clues that let you know you are feeling threatened or hurt emotionally.

- **Be in touch with your feelings.**

  If you have failed to recognize these physical signs, there is still another way to identify when angry feelings are present (even after a day, a month, or even years). If you catch yourself thinking about revenge, or have memories that trigger anger long after the incident, these are signals that you have not resolved the issue. Just saying to yourself that you have forgotten it, or that it's not important, does not make your anger disappear. Even if the incident is a day old, or older, you can go back and attempt to resolve it, or you can get some help to "let go," especially if the person you are angry with is unavailable.

- **Keep an anger diary.**

  You may find it helpful to keep an anger diary. Are there patterns? Do one or two issues keep resurfacing? When you see your feelings on paper, you may be able to look at the situation more objectively and clearly, and come to understand more about the dynamics of your anger.

- **Identify the cause of your anger.**

  Often we act defensively without stopping to recognize what is being threatened or whether we can handle it. If we feel we have the personal power to deal with the threat, we can respond in a calm, rational manner, thus reducing our stress level and increasing our self-esteem.

The following chart illustrates different responses to a threatening event.

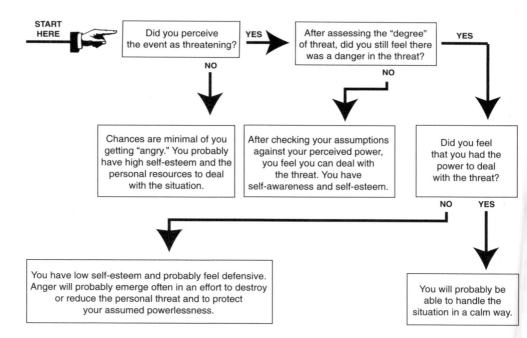

2. *Do not react impulsively.*

Not reacting gives you time to think through the situation and control what you say or do.

- **Evaluate your anger level.**

  Quickly determine just how upset you really are, so you can avoid over-reacting to minor issues or under-reacting to major ones. Anger is not an all-or-nothing response. There are degrees of anger ranging from mild reactions ("I disagree" or "I don't like that" or "I'm bothered") through moderate responses ("I'm annoyed" or "I'm irritated") to intense reactions ("I'm furious"). Learning to differentiate between levels of anger helps you to assess accurately your capacity for dealing with it.

- **Choose your battles.**

  You may even decide to let an incident pass. This does not mean you deny the existence of the problem or the feelings associated with it. It involves a full awareness of the injury done to you and a deliberate decision to drop the issue completely. We must choose our battles. If we don't, we will become critical, negative, and hostile people who fight every issue.

  Ask yourself if your anger is legitimate. Remember that justifying your anger creates more problems. If you catch yourself saying that the other person "made" you angry, you are justifying your anger.

- **Break the habit of reacting defensively.**

  Why is it often hard not to react automatically? Low self-esteem can increase the number of times you feel threatened. You will perceive that you don't have the personal power to deal with the threat, thus you are more likely to react defensively. Once you begin to feel better about yourself, both emotionally and spiritually, you will have less need to be defensive.

3. *Choose how you will deal with anger.*

You may have been able to resolve the problem already by determining that you do not need to respond to a minor issue. However, if the problem is not resolved, here are a few options for taking further action to handle your feelings constructively.

- **Choose not to feel angry.**

  Talk yourself out of feeling angry. Techniques for learning not to react include "counting to 10" and using a "stop" word such as "think" or "breathe." Talk to yourself, using sentences such as "I can work out a plan" or "As long as I remain calm, I'm in control."

145

Develop a relaxation response when you first start feeling angry, such as breathing deeply and slowing the pace of your voice. Speak in a matter-of-fact tone and stick to your point.

- **Talk to the person with whom you are angry.**

  Learn how to express anger assertively. This stops anger from being stuffed by bringing feelings to the surface. You can diffuse the intensity of feelings by speaking openly and honestly. Sharing your feelings clarifies your perceptions and also permits you to receive feedback and validation of your feelings.

  Speaking to the person with whom you are angry does not have to be a hostile, painful experience. What you are trying to accomplish is a direct, non-aggressive communication of your feelings. You do not have to demean or humiliate the other person in the process.

  We should not assume that the other person knows how strongly we feel, unless we express our feelings directly. The use of "I" statements is an assertive way to share your feelings instead of blaming. The expression of these feelings may or may not result in a change in the circumstances which originally caused the anger. Your purpose in confronting is simply to get these feelings out, and to make the other person aware of them.

- **Establish predetermined consequences.**

  Setting predetermined consequences can be used to let others know the limits on their behavior, thus avoiding frustration and hostile situations. The limits should be fair and consistent. All parties must know the consequences before an infraction occurs. The consequences should be logical. For example, if your child does not go to bed when asked once, the logical consequence is an earlier bedtime the next night. This technique reduces power struggles and anger. Establishing predetermined consequences allows you to separate the person from the behavior. In other words, you do not "attack" the person, you address the inappropriate behavior.

- **Set boundaries.**

  Often you may be angry with another person for "using" you. You may feel taken advantage of, and wonder why this keeps happening to you. If you think about it, you are probably angry with yourself for not setting boundaries with others. We teach others how to treat us by letting them know what we will tolerate. You set boundaries by setting limits, by saying no when you mean it, by not feeling responsible for another person's feelings, and by stopping anyone who is physically or verbally abusing you.

- **Agree to a workable compromise.**

We are seldom 100 percent right when we get angry. Often, after going through some of the steps for handling anger, especially talking to the person with whom we are angry, we become aware of the other person's feelings and suddenly are faced with a different perspective on the issue.

A workable compromise is one that is partly fair to both parties. This means that you may not get everything you want, but are willing to take into consideration the other person's needs. The ability to compromise is an integral characteristic of the emotionally and spiritually mature person. It calls for at least a partial sacrifice of deeply held views and goals in order to reach an agreement.

- **Become "other-centered," not "self-centered."**

This is a spiritual process that involves compassion: letting go of the need to be right or always in control, letting down your defenses long enough to hear the other person, and perhaps even asking for help from a higher power to guide you in the process.

You can practice becoming other-centered by listening with your heart and learning to forgive. This step in dealing with anger is probably the most crucial one. At times, we need to fully recognize that although the other person was definitely wrong, we nevertheless choose to forgive and forget. It does not mean that we have to say, "It doesn't matter." It also does not mean that the party at fault does not have to suffer the natural or lawful consequences of his or her actions. Forgiving is a noble gesture that increases personal power and opens you to future transactions.

Being self-centered (overly-concerned for self) only fosters fear. Trusting that you are okay as a person frees you up to be emotionally available to another person, and allows you to be present to someone else's anger without owning it.

Trusting that you are okay as a person frees you up to be emotionally available to another person, and allows you to be present to someone else's anger without owning it.

THIRTY-NINE

The Anger of Others

We often feel defensive when we hear anger. It may be that the child inside us is saying, "What have I done wrong?" and making us feel guilty for no reason.

Like managing your own anger, responding appropriately to the anger of others requires practice and determination. Using the following techniques will help you to develop the skills you need.

1. Do not react immediately.

- **Distance yourself emotionally.**

  Breathe deeply. Imagine an invisible screen in front of you that allows you to hear the other person without "absorbing" his or her anger. This will give you time to determine what the anger is about.

- **Clarify the source of anger.**

  We often feel defensive when we hear anger. It may be that the child inside us is saying, "What have I done wrong?" and making us feel guilty for no reason. The child within feels scared and vulnerable. You can break this reaction by being assertive and asking directly if the person is angry at you. He or she may be frustrated at someone or something totally unrelated to you, and may not even recognize it.

2. Choose how you will respond.

- **Tune out provocation.**

  Although others cannot "make" us angry unless we choose to let them, there may be times when people will try to stir up feelings and push our buttons on purpose. The reasons may be numerous—to feel powerful, to get a desired outcome, or to release their own anger by inciting yours. You can deflect their anger by recognizing the manipulation and tuning out. As you learned earlier,

148

an assertive technique for handling provocation is to agree with the statements. For example, someone says, "You're so messy." You respond by agreeing, "Maybe I am messy." You are not putting yourself down, but letting the comment "run off," like water from a duck's back.

Do not respond to another person's anger with threatening behavior. Avoid getting hooked into what is essentially someone else's problem.

- **Trust your observations.**

  In some situations, the other person may deny that he or she is angry. The first step in dealing with people who look, sound, and act angry, but deny it, is to trust what you see, hear, and feel. For example, you might say, "I see that you're very upset and I am here if you want to talk about it." They will probably say, "I'm not angry" (as they slam the cupboard door shut). Don't get hooked into attempting to pry the reason for the anger out of them, or to "fix" the situation by trying harder to cheer them up. Trust that when, and if, people want to talk, they will! Go about your day being as happy as you want. Don't fall into the trap of being only as happy as they are. You will only be teaching them that they can control your feelings.

- **Leave a high-risk situation.**

  I would like to make something very clear about dealing with another person's anger. Verbal or physical abuse should never be tolerated. You have the right to tell an abusive person to stop. You may wish to add that you are willing to talk when they are more calm (if appropriate). You are completely within your rights to leave an abusive situation.

- **Have a plan.**

  Our buttons get pushed when we are caught off-guard emotionally. The first step is to identify those people and circumstances that upset us. Clue into the physical and mental signals described in the first section of this chapter. Developing a plan puts us in control and allows us to respond effectively. Under-responding or over-reacting can make us feel angry. We are angry at ourselves for letting someone hurt us again, or angry at others for taking advantage of us again. Practice friendly, relaxed responses when you sense a button is being pushed.

- **Reframe your perceptions.**

  Try to see people in a different light. Instead of assuming they are behaving in ways to hurt you or make you angry, realize that sometimes it is the only way they know how to react in a stressful situation. Listen not to the angry words, but to the feeling behind the words. Do you hear stress? Pain? Hurt?

The more you understand about anger, the less power you give it to scare you.

3. Develop personal strengths.

• **Increase self-esteem.**

It is a well-known fact that the better you feel about yourself, the more likely you are to perceive yourself as having the ability to handle your emotional world, to ask for what you need, and to express your feelings without fearing abandonment or ridicule.

• **Learn more about anger.**

Read about anger. Read about assertiveness. Read about family dynamics. Read anything about self-improvement. The more you understand about anger, the less power you give it to scare you. Informing yourself helps to normalize your experience, allowing you to put things in perspective.

• **Develop a sense of humor.**

Look for humor in situations. Laugh at yourself—don't take yourself so seriously. You will be far less sensitive and critical of yourself and others. Understanding that you are only human gives you room for error, and makes risk-taking a whole lot easier. Ask yourself, "What is the worst that could happen?" Life is too short—get a mitt and get in the game!

IN CONCLUSION

The discussions in this chapter are summarized in the chart on the following page. These steps are helpful guidelines in dealing with anger. It is important to experiment and discover what works best for you.

If you find that the anger or problem continues despite your efforts to work it through on your own, the help of a professional may be appropriate.

Steps in Dealing with Anger

Your Own Anger

Step 1: Recognize that you are angry.	Step 2: Do not react impulsively.	Step 3: Choose how you deal with anger.
Own your anger. Develop early warning signs. Be in touch with your feelings. Keep an anger diary. Identify the cause of your anger.	Evaluate your anger level. Choose your battles. Break the habit of reacting defensively.	Choose not to feel angry. Talk to the person with whom you are angry. Establish predetermined consequences. Set boundaries. Agree to a workable compromise. Become "other-centered."

The Anger of Others

Step 1: Do not react immediately.	Step 2: Choose how you will respond.	Step 3: Develop personal strengths.
Distance yourself emotionally. Clarify the source of anger.	Tune out provocation. Trust your observations. Leave a high-risk situation. Have a plan. Reframe your perceptions.	Increase self-esteem. Learn more about anger. Develop a sense of humor.

WORKSHEET: Dealing with Anger

1. Identify some factors that usually trigger your anger. (Consider, for example, moods, certain people or events, disappointments.)

2. List circumstances in which you get hooked into someone else's anger.

3. What can you do instead of getting angry?

4. Describe an event that you are still angry about.

5. Are you over-reacting or justifying your anger?

6. List two things you can do instead of your current anger action:

   Changes in your thoughts

   Changes in your behavior

7. How will these new methods affect others?

8. How will your new methods affect you?

9. How can you reduce your anger level on a regular basis?

12

Strategies for Long-Term Anger Management

FORTY

Making Healthy Lifestyle Choices

There are several "ingredients" that make a good recipe for a healthy lifestyle. Wise people know their skills and limitations, and make the best decisions based on those factors. The following are tips for increasing your chances of feeling in charge of your environment.

The first step in taking charge of your life may be to make a commitment not to give up.

Be consistent and patient.

We have discussed many behavior changes and attitude changes that will help you gain control of your emotional world, enhance your ability to get your needs met, and thus increase your happiness. But change takes time! Expect that people will question and perhaps even fear your new-found openness. You may feel that you are getting nowhere at first. The first step in taking charge of your life may be to make a commitment not to give up.

Increase your choices—try new behaviors.

Anger is not the "problem," but a symptom of the use of ineffective behaviors to get what you want, and perhaps misperceptions based on fears and negative experiences in the past. Taking charge of your life involves increasing your choices about how you will handle situations, and being more in touch with your needs. If you try a new behavior that didn't work as well as you thought it would, use the experience to learn more about yourself and others.

Trust yourself.

Trust what you see, feel, and hear. When you don't, reality gets distorted, and that can make you feel more insecure. When you trust your feelings, you are less likely to deny they exist. Trust that you will be able to

157

Taking control of your life and your needs is important to your happiness.

take care of yourself. You will become more angry if you rely on others to tell you how you feel, or what your reality is. Their perceptions of your reality may be wrong, or they may deliberately mislead you in order to meet their need to dominate or control you.

Maintain a healthy lifestyle.

Good health habits, proper diet, rest, relaxation, fun, and exercise are essential. Taking control of your life and your needs is important to your happiness. People who have positive pursuits in their lives have less time and fewer reasons to be angry than those who are stuck in a rut.

Have realistic self-expectations.

Sometimes we expect too much of ourselves and become angry when we can't accomplish what we set out to do. We may have a need to please others (to feel a greater sense of self-worth), or we may feel inadequate or insecure and push ourselves too far. Some people find it difficult to know when they have done well, or to set realistic limits. Accepting ourselves, our assets, and our liabilities is fundamental to overcoming destructive anger.

Increase self-esteem.

How can you increase your self-esteem? Start by being around people who help you feel good about yourself, people who won't judge you and can give you unconditional love. Make a list of these people. You will find that your anxiety level drops dramatically when you are around them because you are not "on trial."

Another thing that helps self-esteem is to send positive messages to yourself, as this affects how you evaluate your worth.

There is a direct correlation between our feelings of inadequacy or inferiority and the anger in our lives. The bottom line is this: the better we feel about ourselves, the less likely we are to feel bitter, jealous, or defensive. If we feel inadequate and inferior, we will be on guard against anything that threatens our feelings of self-worth, and will protect ourselves with angry counter-attacks.

Learn how to forgive.

You will be able to work yourself into a rage by remembering in detail the incidents that hurt you if you don't learn to let go and forgive. You may also need to forgive yourself. Forgiveness sets you free from the past and reduces the total amount of anger in your life because you don't let anything accumulate. It allows you, consciously and unconsciously, to focus on the present, which leads to more effective and rewarding living.

Focus on your goals.

Working towards any goal takes consistent behavior, and the belief that the outcome will be worth it. This may require a big shift from negative to positive thinking. You will be more able to deal effectively with the hurt, frustration, and fear in your life if you can set and meet your long-term goals.

One way to make it easier to accomplish your life goals is by refusing to see yourself solely as a victim of external events. Even though you may not have much control in your current environment, you are always in charge of your inner world. Believing this will greatly reduce the number of external events that seem threatening. When you feel less threatened, you will probably be able to evaluate your personal strengths and weaknesses more realistically. Once you recognize your own strengths, you may be able to change or leave an unhealthy situation in which your personal goals cannot be achieved.

Remember that your own anger is a powerful source of energy which, if creatively and appropriately expressed, can lead to personal growth and improve interpersonal functioning.

Even though you may not have much control in your current environment, you are always in charge of your inner world.

159

WORKSHEET: Self-Care

Taking charge of your life involves taking care of all your needs. Fill in the following chart, outlining your personal needs and how and when you will fulfill them.

EMOTIONAL NEEDS

(spirituality, time-out, counseling)

_____

_____

_____

_____

_____

_____

SOCIAL NEEDS

(friendship, fun, freedom)

_____

_____

_____

_____

_____

_____

PHYSICAL NEEDS

(health, nutrition, exercise)

_____

_____

_____

_____

_____

_____

PERSONAL GROWTH

(courses, further assessment)

_____

_____

_____

_____

_____

_____

WORKSHEET: Problem-Solving

One example is suggested for each problem. Add as many solutions as you can.

PROBLEM AREAS	NEW THOUGHTS AND BEHAVIORS
1. Negative self-talk	Praise yourself for trying.
2. Receiving compliments	Breathe, say "Thank you."
3. Not trusting feelings	Trust what you see, feel, and hear.
4. Not expressing feelings	Go ahead, your feelings are important.
5. High expectations	Self-worth lies in who you are, not what you can do.

6. Compulsive behaviors   Think about what you really want.

_____

_____

_____

7. Avoiding problems.   Decide what needs to be done and what can wait.

_____

_____

_____

8. Anger from others   Breathe; you do not have to react.

_____

_____

_____

9. Asking for help   Trust people to say no if they can't help you.

_____

_____

_____

10. Feeling hurt   Tell the person who hurt you.

_____

_____

_____

FORTY-ONE

When You Learn to Manage Your Anger

1. You are more able to deal effectively with hurt, frustration, and fear.

2. You don't see yourself as a victim of external events; you are "behind the steering wheel."

3. You are in charge of your inner world. The number of external events that seem threatening is greatly reduced. Feeling less threatened, you will probably be able to evaluate your personal strengths and weakness more realistically.

4. You realize that anger is a powerful source of energy, which, if creatively and appropriately expressed, leads to personal growth and improves interpersonal functioning.

5. You realize that you have choices. You can cope with your problems or be overwhelmed and out of control.

6. You can experience happiness and serenity.

You can experience happiness and serenity.

I'll be nice. I'll give him another hour. That shell of his only weighs him down. Poor guy!

Hey, I don't need to hide behind this shell. It's only for protection when I need it. I'll just put one foot out in front of the other, until I get to the finish line!

HARE & TORTOISE RACE SPECIAL NEXT 3 HOURS

163

REFERENCES

Campbell, Anne. *Men, Women, and Aggression*. New York: HarperCollins, 1993.

Carle, Bev. "The Boat People." Unpublished story, Edmonton, Alberta, 1986.

Clayman, Charles B., ed. *The American Medical Association Encyclopedia of Medicine*. New York: Random House, 1989.

Fletcher, Elizabeth. "Disruptive Feelings: Diffusing Anger in Adolescents." *The Adolescent Counsellor*, January 1992, 35–38.

Hurwitz, Diane, producer. *Anger*. Mississauga, Ont.: Marlin Motion Pictures, 1990. Videotape.

Kübler-Ross, Elisabeth. *On Death and Dying*. New York: HarperCollins, 1969.

Nielson, L. A. *Victims as Victimizers: Therapeutic and Professional Boundary Issues*. New York: Haworth Press, 1990.

Powell, Janet E., and Daniel Taylor. "Anger, Depression, and Anxiety Following Heroin Withdrawal." *International Journal of the Addictions* 27, no. 1 (1992): 25–35.

Spooner, Alan, ed. *The Oxford Study Thesaurus*. Oxford: Oxford University Press, 1994.

ADDITIONAL RESOURCES

Alberti, Robert E., and Michael L. Emmons. *Your Perfect Right: A Guide to Assertive Living*. San Luis Obispo, Calif.: Impact Publishers, 1989.

Canadian Mental Health Association. *Coping with Everyday Problems*. Edmonton, Alberta: Author, n.d.

Canadian Mental Health Association. *Youth and Anger*. Edmonton, Alberta: Author, n.d.

Glasser, William. *Take Effective Control of Your Life*. New York: HarperCollins, 1984.

Lacks, Hazel. "Anger and the Recovering Substance Abuser." *Alcoholism Treatment Quarterly* 5, no. 3/4 (1988): 37–51.

Potter-Efron, Ronald T., and Patricia S. Potter-Efron. "Anger as a Treatment Concern with Alcoholics and Affected Family Members." *Alcoholism Treatment Quarterly* 8, no. 3 (1991): 31–46.

Richard, S. *Releasing Anger*. Center City, Minn.: Hazelden Foundation, 1985.

Rosellini, Gayle, and Mark Worden. *Of Course You're Angry: A Family Guide to Dealing with the Emotions of Chemical Dependence*. San Francisco: Harper & Row, 1985.

Rubin, Theodore I. *The Angry Book*. New York: Scribner's, 1972.

Satir, Virginia. *Peoplemaking*. Mountain View, Calif.: Science and Behavior Books, 1972.

Tavris, Carol. *Anger*: The Misunderstood Emotion (rev. ed.). New York: Simon & Schuster, 1989.

Walfish, Steven, Renelle Massey, and Anton Krone. "Anxiety and Anger among Abusers of Different Substances." *Drug and Alcohol Dependence* 25 (1990): 253–256.

Warren, Neil C. *Make Anger Your Ally: Harnessing One of Your Most Powerful Emotions*. Brentwood, Tenn.: Wolgemuth and Hyatt, 1990.

Weisinger, Hendrie. *Dr. Weisinger's Anger Workout Book*. New York: Quill, 1985.

Woititz, Janet G. *Struggle for Intimacy*. Pompano Beach, Florida: Health Communications, 1985.

For additional copies of Dealing with Anger, *please contact your local bookstore.*

For your convenience, you may also order this book plus additional anger resources by contacting:

BOOK CLEARING HOUSE

1-800-431-1579

All major credit cards accepted, Monday to Friday, 7 a.m. to 5 p.m. EST

E-mail: BCHOUSE@delphi.com   Fax: (914) 835-0015

The following are just a few additional anger resources that can be ordered through the BOOK CLEARING HOUSE:

Other related *Dealing with Anger* manuals, anger merchandise, or for those agencies wanting to purchase copyright to develop their own anger workshops, or work individually with women, please ask for *Dealing with Anger: A Training Manual for Professionals Helping Women.*

To review all anger resources before ordering, please visit the following web site: http//www.xpress.ab.ca/~dcs/

To arrange author interviews, lectures, or special events, please contact the publisher at:

SL DISCOVERY CONSULTING SERVICES INC.

Phone: (403) 459-9570   Fax: (403) 460-5422

For copies of *Miracles for the Entrepreneur*, by Nattalia Lea (the illustrator for this book), or to arrange for joint interviews, please phone:

BOOK CLEARING HOUSE

1-800-431-1579

See next page to order directly from the publisher.

Published by:

SL Discovery Consulting Services Inc.,
16 Marchand Place, St. Albert, Alberta, CANADA T8N 1L8

Phone: (403) 459-9570   **SL Discovery Consulting Services Inc.**   Fax: (403) 460-5422

Women's Health Knowledge Centre
1441 – 29 Street NW
Calgary, Alberta   T2N 4J8
Tel: (403) 944-2267